The Black Writers' Toolbox

The Black Writers' Toolbox

A Practical Guide to Writing Fiction

MULI AMAYE

BLOOMSBURY ACADEMIC
LONDON • NEW YORK • OXFORD • NEW DELHI • SYDNEY

BLOOMSBURY ACADEMIC
Bloomsbury Publishing Plc, 50 Bedford Square, London, WC1B 3DP, UK
Bloomsbury Publishing Inc, 1359 Broadway, New York, NY 10018, USA
Bloomsbury Publishing Ireland, 29 Earlsfort Terrace, Dublin 2, D02 AY28, Ireland

BLOOMSBURY, BLOOMSBURY ACADEMIC and the Diana logo are trademarks
of Bloomsbury Publishing Plc

First published in Great Britain 2026

A catalogue record for this book is available from the British Library.

A catalog record for this book is available from the Library of Congress.

ISBN: HB: 978-1-3504-4476-8
       PB: 978-1-3504-4477-5
       ePDF: 978-1-3504-4478-2
       eBook: 978-1-3504-4479-9

Typeset by RefineCatch Limited, Bungay, Suffolk
Printed and bound in Great Britain

For product safety related questions contact productsafety@bloomsbury.com.

To find out more about our authors and books visit www.bloomsbury.com
and sign up for our newsletters.

This book is dedicated to Black writers, and to our Black
characters in all their authenticity.

Contents

Preface

Our stories have always been told. We are not new to this game of storytelling. Our ancestors weaved our histories through oral stories and these have fed our souls for generations. With the transfer of our storytelling to the page, there are challenges that we, as Black writers, have to face from representation to publication. We also must negotiate creative writing programmes whether these are within education, community or online settings. We need to negotiate with non-Black participants in workshops and often even the facilitators. Just as in life, we are asked to justify why our Black characters do what they do.

I have been teaching creative writing in tertiary education and in the community since 2003. This means I have an opinion on how Black writing and writing Black characters is undertaken. The way in which we approach the page as Black writers, matters. It is different and therefore needs a different approach. Some think it shouldn't matter. As writers we write. We tell our stories, and our audience/ reader connects, or they don't. However, this isn't quite true for Black writers. Within classrooms where there is only one Black writer, it starts to matter when the lecturer or the facilitator starts to question why your character just walked into the room and didn't, you know, kind of shuffle hop into the room. Or your classmate just doesn't believe that your character would spend time finding the owner of a wallet and hand it back intact. While little Johnny in their own story was allowed to steal a purse, whilst thumping the owner, who happened to be an eighty-year-old woman, but then feel remorse and apologise and eventually do the right thing. And let's not forget that overexcitement of finding out that our Black characters 'actually really and truly do that normal thing, and wow, I never knew they could do that'. An exaggeration, but I have been in these types of classrooms as both a student and a lecturer.

It is out of these experiences that this book was born. It will concentrate on Black writing and the theme will be a consideration of how we write ourselves and by extension teach that writing. I use the term 'Black' to encompass any writer who is not white and how the approach to writing can assist in decolonizing the creative writing classroom. However, within this book I am writing as a writer of mixed African heritage and my concentration with the examples used will be on writers of African and Caribbean heritage. There will be very ordinary instruction within these pages. Instruction that can apply to any writer, but that Black writers will understand with a different context. I purposefully concentrate on allowing writers to write their experiences as writers and not simply as 'Black' writers.

The world of literature is changing, slowly, and there are many more Black writers visible, winning major prizes and being recognized nationally and internationally. This is the ideal time for us to consider how we write ourselves and where we are positioned in terms of our writing.

Bob Marley sang that we need to emancipate ourselves from mental slavery. Teaching creative writing makes me think of this sentiment. Often, not always, my students have written themselves into the margins, almost afraid to be heard and be seen on the page. Stereotypes taken from the literature they have read or movies they have seen are at the forefront of their minds. Fortunately, there are contemporary Black writers who are challenging this stereotype and presenting characters who are fully rounded, with all the complexities that involves. If postcolonialism encouraged movement from the margins to the centre for Black characters, what does that look like? It must take into consideration historical, social, situational and psychological spaces.

When I was teaching in the UK my practice had its own set of issues. Often the students were white middle/upper class and had little or no experience of other races or cultures on a deep level. This meant that when students did write other it was without any consideration of characters being fully functional. It was strictly aggressive and subservient Black males and promiscuous Black females described by their body parts. Of course, young writers can write like this for all characters; however, my students' white characters would rarely be stereotypes and would be allowed to explore being human.

These experiences of teaching helped me to grow my practice so that rather than feeling frustrated or upset at what was being produced, I learned to challenge quietly and give full explanations of what and why characters or situations needed to change. This helped me to develop a way of offering learning that assists the students to produce work that is more authentic.

As the world has tried to show solidarity and equity since the killing of George Floyd, which, due to the fact of it being filmed, was as high profile as the beating of Rodney King all those years ago, there has been another call to decolonize, whether this is the curriculum, television and movies, businesses and anything else that holds onto the old ways of being. Is this enough and will it have an impact on the way in which we present ourselves on the page?

Being Black makes it harder to negotiate a world that is predisposed to seeing anyone who is non-white as 'other'. I am aware that 'other' includes many characters, including those who are LGBTQIA+, non-able bodied and many more occupied spaces; however, I am concentrating on writing based around race and colour. Most of the exercises I use can easily be translated for any writing by students outside of their lived experiences, but I will look at the ways in which I approach my teaching and the areas that are very specific to being a writer or teacher of writing that deals with non-white characters.

There are reasons why this approach is necessary. Norrel London (2006) notes that the overall goal of the English curriculum in colonial times was to produce students to be good colonial subjects. Using English language was a priority subject, as a tool for enforcing British sensibilities on colonized people. One of the main tools in decolonizing the classroom is by using Cultural Literacy, which was first defined by Hirsch in the 1980s and was not necessarily received favourably. My definition of Cultural Literacy is having an analytical and critical awareness of the cultural markers within a text, music, art or piece of writing. It is acknowledging and deciphering that there is a culture and a context attached to, say, a piece of literature that needs to be decoded to fully understand its meaning.

Cultural Literacy is used without thinking in the teaching of creative writing, and to decolonize the classroom, creative writing is probably one of the easier ways to explore this concept and works for both undergraduates and postgraduates. When I am teaching, language is one of the markers that needs to be addressed within the classroom. Teaching undergraduates' poetry, for example, I will give the students different exercises for them to gain the tools to write their poetry. Inevitably, the students will begin to write in standard English. I have had students who write about snow and winter, although they have never left their Caribbean island that has two seasons, dry and wet. This shows how ingrained other cultures have become and can be seen to overshadow the student's own culture.

I deliberately set exercises that force the students to take note of what is around them. To give value to their own experiences. At some point during the semester, I have the students write a sonnet, but before that we will do exercises around local language. I will have them work in groups and find all the words that are intrinsically local and be ready to have explanations for them. I often get them to delve deeper than a cursory explanation, looking for the origins of the word, how it fits into a sentence, who it could be used in the presence of. Once this has been explored fully, I will have the students use the form of the sonnet to write a poem using Creole words, using their own everyday ordinary language. For some students, this is a release from having to use standard English to describe something when in Creole one word could describe the whole scenario. This is an ideal way to move away from colonized classrooms. It is simple and effective. Some students, those from the high-ranking schools, who were top of the class, find it extremely difficult to write in Creole because they were not brought up speaking it and feel that it has negative connotations. And this works just as well because these students are then given the task of creating a sense of place using standard English with Caribbean descriptions, so that when I read their work I am located on the island.

There are many 'how to' books for creative writing. I used them when I started teaching and found them to be invaluable. One of my favourites has always been *The Creative Writing Coursebook* by Julia Bell and Paul Magrs. The explanations and exercises offered are well thought out. However, from what I can remember, there is nothing specific for writers of colour, not any in depth consideration of how we approach the page. And I don't think there should be. I'm not here to say that every time an instructional book is written it must apply to everyone who is writing. The books would become tomes, and nobody has the desire to wade through that. I do think that, as educators, we must encourage our students to consider something outside of the standard offerings and that it is important to do it well and properly.

I've used *The Art of Fiction* by David Lodge. This was useful when I was doing my own writing and when I am teaching. In fact, I still refer to the teenage skaz chapter when I am teaching voice, though not in isolation. The examples used in that book don't offer a wide variety of writing, that is, by non-white authors. And that's okay. There is nothing to say it must, and whatever we use in our teaching and writing can be adapted for our own interests and perspectives.

In her 1988 paper, *Unspeakable Things Unspoken: The Afro-American Presence in American Literature*, Toni Morrison addressed the lack of acknowledgement of literature that was written by people of colour, stating that 'There is something called American literature that, according to conventional wisdom, is certainly not Chicano literature, or Afro-American literature, or Asian-American, or Native American', and this can easily be translated to what happens with literatures in English that are by non-white writers. Once a Black person writes a novel that gets into the press, race or ethnicity is brought into the mix. When can a writer be a writer and not an African, Asian, Caribbean or 'other' writer?

One of the main tasks we have as writers and teachers is to fight stereotypes. From movies that are watched to books we read and to people we see on the streets emulating what they have seen in movies, it is a constant battle to present ourselves fully.

The complexities of the human condition are played out constantly in the Caribbean as in the rest of the world. One of the main drivers I have found whilst working in Trinidad and Tobago is religion. Some people here spend a lot of time in church. They work hard, they are educated, have nice houses, drive nice cars, strive for a better life for their children. Chimamanda Ngozi Adichie gave a lecture about the danger of a single story. Of offering one perspective on the lives of Africans, and this can be applied to the Caribbean.

One of the lessons I do with my students is writing 'other'. And by writing other they come to understand that if they are publishing outside of the Caribbean, which is likely they will have to, every character they present on the page is other. There is often resistance from students to the idea that they are presenting stereotypes, but when questioned and probed about their characters and the situations they are in, we start to peel back the layers of the self-limiting beliefs the students hold. Starting with listing the things we know about a certain group of people, we then attempt to uncover where the beliefs stem from.

I ask students to think of themselves as characters and to work out what balance of power they hold within the family, community, church, school, society in general. This is an uncomfortable discussion to have, but it is crucial when thinking about how we write other. I then encourage them to define themselves as fully functional three-dimensional characters.

One of the best parts of the discussion is around how white people are viewed by people from pre-colonized countries. I am provocative in that I suggest that there is a history that was politically, racially and brutally undertaken by the *majority* of white people in the West against pretty much everyone else in the world. Once the students begin to think about this and more than likely agree, I say but it wasn't the *majority* of white people. During the colonial period, the majority of white people were scraping a living doing menial jobs, had no schooling, were not involved in any decisions taken by the higher powers, whether that was Parliament or the monarchy. Certainly, at the beginning of world exploration and domination by the West.

Should all white people be taken as the same in that case? And if most white people were not in a high position, why are all white people assumed to be at the top of the population pile? This is about power. And human nature. Power affects every aspect of a person's life and by extension our character's lives. Every character is affected by and has a relationship with power. There must be consideration given to the balance of power that is at play within the characters' situation. It's true that poor white people had no power while others were running around colonizing the world; the power deficiency, however, was economic, class driven. Intersectionality comes into play for a Black character and therein lies the immediate differences within the writing.

It is an uncomfortable discussion to be had, but it is important as writers that we get it right. This is the type of teaching in the creative writing classroom we need to get comfortable having if there are to be changes. We must challenge the students and ourselves because when we get it wrong on the page, we are failing the craft of writing and failing our students.

I was invited by Midnight & Indigo, a literary magazine and publishing company dedicated to celebrating the voices of Black women writers worldwide, to run workshops for a cohort of African American women called the Black Women Writers' Toolbox. I entered a space where the women could write their stories without explanation. They could make a flippant comment about something that is specifically a Black experience, and there were nods of assent. There was nobody to say, well that doesn't really happen, or to challenge it being a Black experience when it could be seen as universal. There are subtleties and underlying knowledge that Black writers carry and as educators we don't get to tell them that their writing is wrong or that it isn't authentic. I am not African American, so I don't understand all the complexities of living within that society, but growing up in the United Kingdom can provide me with some type of common ground.

Creating a space where writers can explore their craft authentically is crucial if there is going to be a decolonization process both in the classroom and in the publishing industry. This is not only relevant to writers of colour; we don't only decolonize for Black students but for all students. Think about the assumptions that are made about characters when there are no markers to indicate that the character is non-white. They are just characters doing character things within a setting and a plot.

We don't want to introduce conflict into the classroom around race just because we think we should; we want to do it because it's good practice. Whilst teaching in the United Kingdom, I didn't articulate to myself about decolonizing the classroom, but looking back it was something I did naturally. So how can this be done with a class of first-year undergraduate students who are writing what they know? How about deconstructing the characters they write about? Not only in terms of writing a character profile; best friends, childhood illnesses, parents, school, height, hair colour, body type, gender, sexual orientation. While those are items that naturally go into a character profile, we can take it deeper. We can encourage the students to think about what shaped the characters' way of thinking beyond the family. What beliefs do the characters hold that they assume are innate, but are in fact social constructs? What happens when they put that character in an unfamiliar space with other characters who are not like them? We can gain an understanding of privilege due to skin colour through our white characters without having the binary of a Black or brown character to compare to.

Similarly, when we are thinking about language, there are ways in which to show different *Englishes* on the page without them being written in such a way that the narrator sounds uneducated. Trying to capture the musicality of another language is difficult, but not impossible. Even without another character explaining how their friend speaks in a sing-song accent.

Also thinking about language, I have students who use the 'N' word or slip in the word 'Coolie' if they are Indo-Caribbean. These students will argue that it's okay for the characters to refer to themselves in this way because they are reclaiming the word, making it their own. This is a great argument, because now we can deconstruct where the word came from in its derogatory state. And once that is unpicked, the students understand that they are not claiming back anything that was theirs but are using a slur that was levied against their people in a particular era.

I use these illustrations to show that decolonizing the classroom is not something that is only applicable when teaching in British universities, but also in pre-colonized countries where students see themselves through another's gaze.

Whilst attempting to decolonize the creative writing classroom, I will probe and question decisions made by students when writing about themselves or others within their society and tell the students that they must do better and not fall into the trap of othering that is so often offered in the Western texts they have studied. This act alone begins to decolonize the students' minds and the classroom setting and offers a depth of cultural literacy that is invaluable in producing students with a strong sense of self-worth in their identity. This book is born out of the desire to help Black writers understand their position on the page and to fully embrace all the complexities of a Black character.

For those interested in furthering knowledge and conversation around decolonizing the creative writing classroom, there are books available. Two examples are *The Anti-Racist Writing Workshop: How to Decolonize the Creative Classroom* by Felicia Rose Chavez, and *Craft in the Real World: Rethinking Fiction Writing and Workshopping* by Matthew Salesses.

This is a book of craft. A toolbox for Black writers to have something to refer to when they are writing. The point of the book is that it is for expanding our writing knowledge, encouraging us to think about why we write as we write and normalizing us on the page.

Foreword

Black aesthetics as method, politics and beauty

Mukoma Wa Ngugi

'I have had students who write about snow and winter, although they have never left their Caribbean Island that has two seasons, dry and wet'

MULI AMAYE

The Black Writers' Toolbox: A Practical Guide to Writing Fiction calls us in for an urgent conversation.

What happens when we put white aesthetics aside and really think about what Black aesthetics exist across the diaspora? In mainstream white aesthetics it is the more abstract and unrecognizable the better, with the more grounded being a lesser form. I know this because I did my MA in creative writing at Boston University where I was expected to deracinate the pain of politics from aesthetics – as if the two are mutually exclusive. As if the memory and literary traditions, informed and forged by struggles against slavery, colonialism and neocolonial dictatorships, the same forces that forced my father into detention and exile and left my family in Kenya living in violence and fear, were mere affectations.

This urgent call for a conversation raises a more fundamental question – what happens when Black people in the diaspora really think about what it is about our aesthetics that keeps us in conversation? What are the differences and joys between the kinds of writing we produce in Afro-Latino, Caribbean, African American and continental African spaces?

And what do we with the language, the very DNA of all writing? Do we try and supplant it with standard English, the English we use in various diasporic locations? Dr Amaye's answer is to use the languages you have. So, she advises her students to use 'their own everyday ordinary languages, including Creoles, languages we have that have been forged by generations through our lived experiences. In short, a homegrown aesthetics that comes with language, worldview, our diasporic DNA. We cannot write through 'another's gaze'. Write from where you are.

And then she takes us from the world of theory into the world of practice, of praxis. And she does this by providing examples of writers that in their own different ways capture writing from our own societal DNA.

From words and sentences to larger thematic concerns, she gives us stories and a Black aesthetic reading of a diverse group of Black writers, say Leone Ross, June Aming, Celeste Mohammed, Courttia Newland, Malcolm Cocks and Nii Ayikwei Parkes.

This writing toolbox bravely tackles the question of Black aesthetics outside the frame of white aesthetics by positioning it in the Black diaspora. It makes a case for decolonizing Black aesthetics, the writing classroom and, more importantly, our imagination.

*Mukoma Wa Ngugi is Professor of Literatures in English – Cornell University and the author of *The Rise of the African Novel: Politics of Language, Ownership and Identity*.

Acknowledgements

First, I would like to acknowledge and thank the senior commissioning editor at Bloomsbury, Lucy Strong, who saw the importance in our writing and our work and envisioned this book; and Aanchal Vij, who guided me to the finishing post.

Writing this book would not have been possible without all the writers and teachers who have helped me to hone my craft authentically. Without the Commonword novelists writing group led by Peter Kalu, I would not have known there was a space for me to write without censorship or questioning. Professor Graham Mort at Lancaster University helped me to understand my own writing and to be unafraid to make my characters take up space on the page.

All the writers who have generously given their time and their stories to be part of this project have made it possible for this book to be born. I thank you for your dedication to the craft and to other writers.

How to use this book

Most chapters and exercises in this book can be seen in other creative writing 'how to' manuals. The difference with this book is that from the title to the introduction, you are being informed that we are looking at writing from a different perspective. We are valuing the alternatives of where we sit on the page as Black writers or with Black characters. Although the exercises can be used by any writer, I have purposely added the word Black into each chapter title to remind us that we are allowed to write our stories without stressing Blackness – unless we choose to!

The chapters follow a natural progression, if we treat them as a writing course, or they can be dipped into in any order as need be.

Each chapter is laid out pretty much the same way, with an introduction to the topic, examples, discussion suggestions, exercises and a round up.

There are full short stories by Black writers at the end of each chapter and we can use these to look for points that were introduced in the previous chapters. Read them like a writer. Question how the character has been developed, what the setting is telling, concentrate on voice and point of view and decide how they have been employed for the benefit of the story. Revisit the stories at any point and see how all the tools have been used to produce them. If we don't read, we can't write. Approach your reading and your writing in the same way. Questioning, exploring, probing – whatever it takes for you to understand what you're reading and what you're writing.

1

Structuring Black sentences

- How do we define a sentence?

- Deciding how to use sentences in our writing.

- Exercises to practice.

The way in which we structure sentences matters. This chapter will consider the importance of sentence structure when writing to create different feelings in the writing and ultimately responses for the reader. It will touch on the language and syntax difference for people from around the globe rather than assuming all writers are Western and use a particular vernacular.

We can define a sentence according to dictionary definitions. But, as writers know, we play around with words so much, the definitions feel as though they are there to be pulled apart and put back together again upside down and inside out!

Having said that, definitions are a good place to begin though, so what is a sentence?

1 A set of words that is complete in itself, typically containing a subject and predicate, conveying a statement, question, exclamation, or command and consisting of a main clause and sometimes one or more subordinate clauses. (Oxford Dictionary)

2 A word, clause or phrase or a group of clauses or phrases forming a syntactic unity which expresses an assertion, a

question, a comma, a wish, an exclamation, or the performance of an action, that in writing usually begins with a capital letter and concludes with appropriate end punctuation, and that in speaking is distinguished by characteristic patterns of stress, pitch and pauses. (Merriam-Webster)

So, now we can be confused together. Or we can use our sentences in the ways we know how and not stress too much on what they are. We have been told that 'no' is a full sentence. And if 'no' is a full sentence, 'eh-eh' is a full sentence and even a paragraph depending on the character and the context.

> **Jonnie:** *I did see Missy yesterday with that fella. The one who was married and I did hear he wife find out and is looking for she. Missy best watch sheself.*

> **Petey:** *Eh-eh!*

Sentences may seem like a strange place to begin. Everybody knows what a sentence is. We can't write our stories without them. That's how language works on the page. In sentences. Lots of them. One after the other. Until they create a meaning and do what they need to do.

But do we all use sentences to their best advantage in our writing? How many times have you written a story that is meant to be tense, and yet somehow, the tension is missing, and you can never quite work out why because all the words are there, you're writing this thing, and you feel the building tension and you don't know what is going to happen to your character or the situation. Did you notice what I did there? A very long sentence that is about creating tension in our writing. And yet, it meanders across four lines as though it has all day to get to the point.

Writing fiction is more than simply putting sentences together. It's the way we do it that matters. We can't normally create tension with meandering sentences. Imagine your writing as music. When something is about to happen, the music becomes short and sharp. It comes out in bursts. We hold our breath. Tension builds. We need to get that same feeling down on the page. What music would your writing be if it was a warm sunny day cycling through the countryside, with birds singing, sheep in the fields and a picnic date? Or better yet, if you were on the beach, hot white sand between your toes, the ocean clear and calm beckoning you in, children laughing as they chase the waves, a glass of something cool in your hand.

We can learn to use sentences, both in terms of length and word usage, in ways that enhance our writing. We can have one scenario and produce different meanings, using pretty much the same words, but varying the sentence length.

For example:

a) Lisa had completed all her morning chores and was washing up her coffee mug. She was musing about the upcoming meeting in work, but not worried as she had everything prepared. Gathering her bag and lunch, she collected her car keys from the dish on the sideboard in the hallway. Checking her braids in the mirror, she threw a stray one over her shoulder and smiled at their neatness. She opened the door and found him standing there even though he hadn't said he was coming. It was both a shock and a surprise and she laughed out loud involuntarily.

b) Lisa completed her morning chores. She was washing her coffee mug, thinking about the upcoming meeting. She wasn't worried, she'd prepared. Picking up her lunch and bag she grabbed her car keys. Her hair in the mirror was neatly braided. She opened the door. He was standing there. He shouldn't have come. She was shocked. She involuntarily laughed.

Both of those scenarios are saying the same things in different ways. In the first example we would think it was her friend or lover and she was pleased to see him. In the second example we could get the feeling of a stalker or an unwelcome guest. We could feel scared for her reading this in context. Obviously, the wording has changed slightly to fit the mood in the second example. The intention is to show us the power of sentence length. Language would also enhance the emotion of the example:

a) Lisa completed her morning chores. She was washing her coffee mug, thinking about the upcoming meeting. No stress, she'd prepared. Picking up her lunch and bag she grabbed her car keys. Her face in the mirror was strained. She cracked open the door. He was there. She gasped. It became a sob.

These are the extremes of how we use our sentences. Clearly, parts of our writing will be neither languid nor tense. So, what do we do there? We think about how we talk. Often, we vary the length or our sentences. And we do this because otherwise we'd be talking in a monotone and our listeners would zone out. We naturally vary sentence length to retain interest and our writing does the same thing. If you look over something you've written, check your sentences, you will see that you automatically break them up in natural places. There are times when we don't do that and that's where editing comes in. Read your work out loud. Listen to how it sounds. Where do you need to take a breath? Is it in the natural rhythm of how you would speak or listen. This will give you the clues you need as to whether your sentences are working and doing their job.

We don't always write in standard English, and we don't have to. We write in the form of language that our characters, story and plot require. This is important to understand as Black writers or writers with Black characters. The syntax and rhythm of the sentence is not lesser or ill formed if it is in something other than standard English. The rules are the same. You use varied sentence lengths depending on what you want to convey. We will look at the language we use in chapters 5 and 6, and unapologetically use local parlance as a right.

Discussion point

- What is it about sentence length that affects the way we read something and the way we feel about what we've read?

- Can we make up some examples as above and see what happens to our writing?

- Start to take notice in stories you read. How does the writer create the emotions they want us to feel? Count the words in each sentence if you need to. Stop and consider how you are feeling about what you are reading.

Example 1

The grave empty fast: the earth still loose. The sounds of breath in and out. No one talk. He can't even stretch his brain to the evil of what he was doing. Who it was wrap up in the tarp? Who he cross?

AYANNA LLOYD BANWO *When We Were Birds* (2022), 168

This is written in creole and the same rules apply regarding varying sentence length. We can feel the tension rising in the narrator. The author cleverly puts a medium length sentence in the middle – 'He can't even stretch his brain . . .' – which works with what we are reading. There will be times when vernacular is used because that is how a character speaks. The same rules will apply. If we are creating tension, the sentences and the word choices will show it.

Example 2

They continued on through the village, showing the white man the town square, the small fishing boats formed from hollowed-out tree trunks that the men carried with them when they walked the few miles down to the coast.

YAA GYASI, *Homegoing* (2016), 2

In contrast, in the novel *Homegoing*, by Yaa Gyasi, we are given the sense of the journey and of travelling through space and time. We are taken to a particular point in time, during colonialism, in a very simple way. The long sentence sees us walking through the village slowly with the characters and making observations. There is no tension; we are meandering.

Example 3

Here. She could paint this; hold the brush as a stabbing knife. There. Colouring in landscapes of loss. She could draw this for him, this longing to hear his particular voice, listening for echoes of bloodied footsteps, borrowing dead eyes to help her find him again. Here.

YVONNE ADHIAMBO OWOUR, *Dust* (2014), 14

In this example, we can see how tension is building. The short staccato sentences let us take the journey with the character. It's hard to catch breath. We get a strong sense of how the character is feeling even if we don't know what has caused it. It's the equivalent of that music you hear in movies when something is about to happen. The language used for a paintbrush alerts us to the characters' emotional state – a stabbing knife. And then, we are taken on a meander in the middle of it all and it represents the longing of the character and how it is drawn out.

Practising sentence length helps us to understand the impact sentences can have on our writing. As we've established, you will naturally have a balance in your sentences, so for these exercises we are going to extremes. We are practising creating tension and meandering, so that you'll recognize when you need to use the tools of sentence length composition.

Exercise 1

- Write a paragraph about walking through the market at lunchtime on a Saturday. You're not in a rush, you have nowhere to be and are quite relaxed. Describe anything of interest, your thoughts, the smells and the sounds. Don't limit yourself. Use all your experiences of walking through any marketplace you've ever been to, whether these were sanitized indoor markets or loud and sprawling outdoor markets.

- Now rewrite the same paragraph to create tension. It's lunchtime on a Thursday. You only have forty-five minutes for your lunch break and the market is packed. This means you are in a heightened state of tension. Shorten the sentences. What will happen if you're back to work late? Is this the first or the seventh time? Have you had a warning before? Or can you find what you need? What will happen if you don't get it? Let your short sentences and language do the job for you.

Exercise 2

- Take a paragraph from a short story or a chapter of a novel that you have read. If it's full of tension, rewrite it in long sentences, make it languid, let the reader float along the sentences. Change the language as you need to, but stay true to the paragraph you're using.

- If it's already languid and doesn't hold any tension, create it. Make the sentences short and sharp. Change some of the language. Let the ordinary become chilling. Use your imagination freely, you don't have to stick to the script of the story you're using.

Round up

Sentence length will have an impact on how your story is read. Short sharp sentences create tension, whether that is through excitement, fear or anger or any other high emotion. Longer, languid sentences will allow the reader to relax into the scene, whether this is a slow Sunday afternoon or a meandering walk through a village. In between, you will vary your sentence length naturally, just as we do in speech. This will keep the attention of the reader and make sure there isn't a monotone to your work. Be aware of what type of story you want to write. Your sentences will impact how it is read. Use them to your advantage.

Read

Read the following story – 'Velvet Man' by Leone Ross – with your focus on sentence length. Note down when and where you feel the tension rising. Look at the sentence structure and notice how it adds to the telling of the story. There are some very long sentences broken up by colons and semi-colons and sometimes just commas. How does this make you read those sections?

The market was in full swing with mid-morning bargains, the scrape of bottles and boxes, smells of best meat and fish, and she'd never seen the city sky so blue, amplifying every blush in the arcade: melons hacked open, sides of salmon strewn with black peppercorns; strawberry tarts glistening in syrup.

This sentence has me imaging walking through a very busy market. As much as the sentence is long, there is a frenetic feel about it, so it isn't a leisurely stroll through the market, it's done with purpose.

This part gives us some clipped sentences. Not for tension but for her state of mind. For the tightness in her demeanour: 'Just put it back where you found it. Everything in its place. The secret is in the upkeep. Just be organized.'

Take note throughout of where this happens. What are the long sentences telling you and what are the clipped short sentences indicating? How does it add to the reading of the story?

You can come back to this story at any point and pick out the other tools that have been used throughout to create the story.

'Velvet Man'

Leone Ross

Ghosts know who best to haunt. An old Jamaican friend once told her that. She thinks about this idea a lot, after the velvet man leaves. About what it is to be drawn to something just for you: a perfectly fashioned event, a person, or a moment. It is the kind of thing that people write about – this flawless sense of fate – but she'd never understood it. She was a sensible woman. Better to do your nails, steam your face and cook for the week on a Sunday. To read the material two weeks in advance of the meeting, then a few days before to refresh the memory: that was success. To buy pak choi in the local market and better quality cuts of meat at the butcher; extra money-saving lightbulbs; keep numbers for the plumber and the local hot-line for nuisance neighbours by the phone; insure the dog. Iron your skirt, because.

* * *

She was late for work that morning, smoothing her fingers over her knees and her well-ironed blue skirt when the velvet man entered the empty train carriage, sat down right next to her – when he might have taken any of twenty other battered, orange and blue patterned seats available – and murmured something softly under his breath.

She was not troubled in the first few seconds, nor even surprised at his long limbs or his sudden proximity. If forced to say, she might have explained that it felt like an old friend had wandered onto the train, after years of absence, and she'd recognised his saunter or the back of his head.

The man murmured again. His eyes made her think of those black velvet paintings that were all the craze in the seventies. Her mother had kept two in the drawing room, one of John Wayne, the other of five dachshunds playing poker. When she was a child she'd been smacked more than once for pulling a chair up below them so she could stroke their soft edges.

'Pardon me?' she said to the velvet man.

He smiled. She could smell his healthy, wheaty breath, took in his thick, white-blonde hair and his large hands that were spread over his denim knees. She looked down at his clean, well-shaped fingernails. Those eyes: oddly black where you'd really expect blue, given his colouring. She might poke her finger inside and suck something sweet off the tip of it.

'Tell me what I can do for you,' he said.

His face was open; eyes steady and perfectly calm. It was a kind face, and she thought there was a sort of bravery in exposing that to a stranger. She opened her mouth to ask him all the obvious questions – who are you, don't talk to me, move away, what could you possibly mean? She could feel where the muscles in her wrists and thighs should be tensing for movement up out of her seat and away.

Instead, she paused. He was joking, of course. It was mere hyperbole – like those Nigerian men who told you they were princes in their countries; or like a new song that runs out of steam after it started so well.

'Tell me what I can do for you,' the velvet man said patiently.

His expression was solemn, watching her carefully, as if this might be the most important thing he would say today, or this week.

Suddenly, hotly, she considered the idea. The deliciousness, the expansiveness of it assailed her. She could be important, different; she felt a lurching in her chest. She was late on the train, heading for ordinary: the job, the lunch-break, the colleagues, the wishes, the dreams, all so irreparably dull and chipped.

The train pushed into the station and she knew what she wanted – at least, where to begin. She grabbed his hand; he rose up with her, and there was joy on his face.

***

The market was in full swing with mid-morning bargains, the scrape of bottles and boxes, smells of best meat and fish, and she'd never seen the city sky so blue, amplifying every blush in the arcade: melons hacked open, sides of salmon strewn with black peppercorns; strawberry tarts glistening in syrup.

And the peonies at the flower stall.

She came to an abrupt stop in front of them, dropping the velvet man's hand, tucking her palms together like a little girl, teeth in her bottom lip. She was rocking slightly, almost breathless. Her parents had thought cut flowers a bourgeoisie affectation.

She looked up at the velvet man: he was beaming, waiting. 'But of course,' he said. More flowers, she thought later, than anyone had ever got in the world. Armfuls of the pink peonies first, because she liked their little cabbage faces peeping up at her; fat roses next, ringed in sprays of eucalyptus, and the velvet man instructed the flower stall owner to make sure every thorn was taken off. He'd opened his mouth to say you're having a laugh, mate, but then the velvet man gave him enough money to make him grin and set his assistant picking. Urged on by both men now, she chose huge daisies the size of her hand, laughing delightedly; a long box of cerise anthuriums, their bright plasticky stamens reminding her of hot places.

'Happy?' asked the velvet man, when all were chosen and she stood, sticky with sap and ever so slightly breathless at her own excess. She hesitated. He was still smiling, gently leaning down to move a leaf from her hair.

'Yes,' she said. 'Thank you. So generous. Thank you so much.' 'And now . . .?'

His bow was near-genuflection. She stared.

'What?'

'Whatever you want.'

She was the kind of woman who had always paid her way. Paid her half of the meal, despite her date's protests. Not that there had been a million men in her life. She had an ordinary face and an easily concealed body, so there had been no more than a few gently drunken fumbles before Jack, at uni. She knew she could have gathered many more sexual experiences: a plain girl was easy, by necessity. But she was determined not to be seen in that way; invisibility was the better choice.

Jack was bearded and fairly ordinary himself: unexpectedly judicious in his courting. The first time they had sex he lost and gained his erection three times, sawing back and forth inside her so long that his eventual orgasm had them both mistaking relief for love.

***

She wanted to see things, do things, new things. The velvet man slid them into a black car sleek with butter-soft upholstery.

A private viewing of several complex and beautiful paintings, he guiding her from one piece to another, pointing out colour, texture, inviting her thoughts. She knew nothing of modern art, but as he smiled and shared his own pleasure in the work, she slowly began to say what she saw, felt, loved.

The velvet man hired a helicopter so they could zoom low over the city, snug together in the belly of a huge bumblebee, yelling happily over the roar of the blades. Below her, the city looked bleak and cheerless, and she was momentarily frightened, making herself small under the velvet man's armpit. He smoothed the soft hair at her temples and squeezed her hand, yelling almost angrily at the pilot: 'Take us down!'

'No,' she said, 'can we just see something pretty?'

'Close your eyes,' he said, 'I'll tell you when,' and she might have dozed against his chest, or through some deeper reverie, and then the city was behind them and they were to-ing and fro-ing above green hills, watching silver-blue rivers pour deep into tiny valleys. She wondered if they disturbed the birds, and at the softness of the velvet man's skin over his chest and arms.

'Happy?' he asked.

'Yes,' she managed to say, her cold cheek against his good shirt.

'I'll do anything you want,' he said.

***

Jack had broken off with her in the second year, to sleep with a more intelligent woman, she suspected, then come back with his tail between his legs the term afterwards. She'd punished him for just long enough and then they'd stayed up late studying for finals in her neat and polished room – he politics and history, she marketing. They had married two years later; divorced seven years after that. There had been no children, a fact that relieved her nearly as much as the sight of his slightly sweaty-shirted back walking out of their small, well-organized apartment, hands gripping two suitcases she'd refused to pack for him, then packed anyway, and a large teddy bear he'd had since childhood. The divorce was uncomplicated, as such things go.

All the way through their courtship and lives together, she'd had jobs, maintained her own chequing account and independence; paid half the bills. She had decided to be the best of modernity: she would not be hoe or a bitch or a gold-digger or a floozy – or what did they call them these days? Thots and skanks and ratchet girlies. No. That kind of woman offended her. The rampant consumerism even more than the exchange of flesh.

* * *

A spa was next: entry via a discreet doorway off an expensive street. He waited patiently in the quiet foyer as she was taken away and stripped: washed first in sprays of perfumed water, a salt scrub applied, then thick, warm cinnamon oil ladled all over her body and rubbed in; more water to finish; the gentle breathing of the two women working on her tight neck, her loose calves. She had always been thin and relatively fit, but under their ministrations she felt like a crust of something – stale bread, a discarded piece of a pie. A sliver of something they were trying to render pliable.

One of the girls wrapped her in a robe and brought her attention to a tray of jewellery sent in for her, and the security guard beside it. Despite their professionalism, neither masseuse could restrain their giggles – a kind of raw pleasure that scraped against her as she watched them. They nudged her, all girls together, excited. She felt their envy, realised that they were examining her, trying to see what magic she had worked on this man. Where was it – in her pores and crevices, and could they have some, too?

She considered her own feelings as she touched the diamonds. There was a price to be paid, she accepted that. She did not want to think what, but certainly sex. She had never slept with a stranger before; the thought made her feel dull and determined. But she would go with him, and do what he wanted. There was no other ending to the story.

'Your boyfriend says he wants to watch you choose.'

She pulled her robe tight and watched the velvet man come in, through slitted eyes.

***

She had never really kept close friends; the few she did have, from university, and then two colleagues, a man and a woman, all seemed to admire her, but then no more. Jack had been more sociable than she: he had someone over at least once a month to eat the food she cooked and to remark on their flat. Someone had once politely called it a show home, and the praise always left her satisfied.

'Just so,' Jack had said, mimicking her. 'Everything just so. Like you're my fucking mum or something.'

'It doesn't take very much to keep things nice,' she'd argued. 'Just put it back where you found it. Everything in its place. The secret is in the upkeep. Just be organized.'

'I'd like to see you lose your mind, just once,' he said. It was one of the few things he'd ever said with substance; he was no puzzle. But it had surprised her: the force of his wish. Would he have revelled more in her temper or a screaming, undignified orgasm? Or did he want to see her stark staring mad, clawing at the sky?

She'd been glad to see the back of him. Friends of his called to tell her how much they admired her fortitude, her pragmatism; the quiet respect she afforded him during a short period of bitter-mouthed alcoholism, short because well – he was far too judicious to really become a nuisance in anyone's life. He had done his best with her. Just she wore away people, over time. She knew that about herself. She was a transitory experience. Her parents rang infrequently, usually Tuesday, as if they kept a diary somewhere. She was a duty: that was fine.

***

She was shaking by the time they reached her neighbourhood, car inching its way through old buildings like oil. Some arrangement had been made with the market florist and all her pink flowers had been packed carefully, carpeting the floor of the car and overflowing in the back. The driver sneezed. The velvet man stroked her hand. He looked concerned – or was it the grim visage of a man about to claim his pound of flesh? She was horrified. What was the price of this day, of the diamond bracelet on her wrist, its sharp brilliance cutting through the evening gloom?

'Here,' she said. The car slunk into place.

He saw that she was shaking. His face, distressed. 'What can I do?' he said, rubbing and rubbing the back of her thin hand. 'How can I help?' Above them, the balcony of her simple, second-floor apartment loomed.

She turned to face him.

'We have to go somewhere else. I'll do what you say, but not here.'

'I wanted to see your home, full of flowers.'

'Not here,' she hissed. 'No.'

He drew away from her. 'What is it that you think we're going to do?'

She made a gesture, across her body, hand sharp, fingers flailing.

He shook his head, stroked her face.

'You still don't understand. I do what you want. Your pleasure is mine. There is no price.'

She squinted. 'But. . .'

He laughed, low. Seemed softer than ever.

'Whatever you need.'

She could feel her backbone begin to unfurl. Could there be this kind of man? She didn't know how it worked.

He gathered her face in his hands. 'Anything I can do. It's my pleasure.'

The feeling of recognition returned, that there are spirits that know what you are. She felt something tilt inside. She grasped his shoulders, hurting herself, hurting him, perhaps? It didn't matter. All for her. He said so. An impossibility. Let him see her sins.

***

Her nails bite into his wrist, as they walk towards her front door. There is a nest of silver cobwebs in the eaves, a black garbage bag, strewn in the way. She keeps hold of his hand, fits the key with the other, smoothly opens.

The apartment smells of old washing-up and the cheese of mould. There are pieces of discarded clothing in the hall. They traverse the items, she kicking them out of the way. Old candle wax, long-sputtered across bookshelves. Dust everywhere, on alphabetised books and matching crockery. She stands, hands dangling, as he takes it in, looking around him, back to her.

There is a half-eaten chicken leg in the middle of the living room floor. The sofa is stained, with matching stained cushions. Detritus teeters: saucers, each sugared with ancient meals. In the kitchen, piles of dirty clothes totter in front of the sink, the full dishwasher, the full washing machine. She has been washing the same clothes for three days, unable to do more than add new liquid, then sit on the dirty kitchen floor, watching the same items wash again, unable to make herself open the door and take the damp items out and spread them on her balcony, or through the flat to dry. Dotted through the rooms are dusters, including a feather one, spray polish, disinfectant, floor-cleaner, bleach. She has been carrying them around and laying them in piles.

He watches her carefully, nods her on. They are not done.

She has been sleeping on a naked mattress for weeks; it is too much to make the bed at the end of a day. Most of the bed is occupied – half-drunk water bottles among the pillows, hairbands and used tights where she's dragged them off and discarded them. Pills – all her efforts to soothe, improve, heal, take control: Omega-3 supplements, multivitamins, evening primrose oil. A cracked lipstick. There is old vomit down the side of the bed.

The velvet man looks at the flat and looks at her. She is swaying in her shame.

Her mouth cracks open. 'I'm so lonely,' she says.

* * *

Into the night, she listens: to the scud of a broom across wood; the flushing of a toilet; the tamp-tamp sound of fresh sheets being shaken out; jangling clothes-hangers; a scrubbing brush against the floor, the rattle of pill bottles. Bleach, floor polish. He could pay, but he does it with his hands. Sounds of him lifting the bed, the desk, each one of her shoes. Bags of junk, stink, shame, removed. As dark deepens: the striking of a match for candles and incense; the sweet smell of peonies gathered and fluffed; a choice of low music – guitar and drum, and him, humming along; she begins to breathe again; she dozes; wakes to his lips brushing against her forehead; the snicker of the front door opening and closing.

2

Using Black senses

- Explore each of the five senses.

- Read some examples of how the senses can enhance our writing.

- Do some exercises to practise using all the senses.

The senses impact writing and reading and bring the reader into the scene. In this chapter we will explore using the senses in ways that are not stereotypical and that enhance Black writing rather than fall into categories that depict 'Black' behaviours. Often, in an attempt to write Black characters who are acceptable on the page, the senses are downplayed. Characters are not allowed to be fully formed and functional and this can easily slip into stereotype and caricature.

Why does that character react in a particular way in a given situation? Perhaps they smelled an aroma that took them back to childhood, a time when they felt safe and loved. Perhaps the texture of the shirt she is wearing is the same as that of the work colleague who invaded her personal space during a bullying incident. Although it can be argued that it would be the same for any character, irrespective of their race or gender, for Black characters we must be aware of the intersectionality of being. This by default makes everything more extreme. There are micro aggressions that would not be noticed by anyone else, but a Black person picks up on them and they create feelings and emotions and heighten the senses. By using the full range of senses, characters are afforded to be 'human', with all the complexities that involves.

The senses are extremely important for our writing. They draw the reader in and allow them to become part of the story. The way we use them matters because we want to integrate them seamlessly into our writing. And we only use them where they matter: to move the story along and when they are relevant to what is happening. There are several ways to do this, and we'll explore them in this chapter.

Sight

If we are people who can see, our sight is the main way we take information in. Think about it. We look where we are going, we read people's expressions and body language. We appreciate the beauty of a landscape or a painting. We don't enjoy looking at things that are unpleasant, like a raft of litter or plastic on a beach. Our eyes often guide us and take in information that we're not always aware of. Look around where you are right now. If it's a space you're familiar with, the chances are unless something is in a different place or missing, you haven't really taken notice of your surroundings because they're familiar and everything is as it should be. We often rely on sight because we're not used to taking notice of our other senses unless it's something that disturbs us.

Smell

We use our noses and our sense of smell more than we know. If you walk into a room or down a street and there is an unpleasant smell, your nose will let you know. Maybe we forgot to put the rubbish out or we walked past a blocked drain. On the other hand, we may pick up an extremely pleasant smell; I've followed people down the street sniffing them on occasion – don't call the police! Or I've walked past a bakery and that fresh smelling bread has compelled me to go and buy something even though I'm not hungry and don't usually eat bread. What can I say, the sense of smell is quite marvellous when we think about it.

We connect smells to experiences. Imagine walking through an unfamiliar market space and you smell some food cooking. It's a paella and the smell is very distinctive. A few years ago, you were on holiday in Valencia, Spain with your friends. One of them was flirting with the waiter and ended up spending the whole holiday with him. Two years later she's married to him. So, you're standing in a market in the middle of winter in your hometown, wanting to get home and tuck into the soup you made earlier, but you're transported to Spain in the height of summer and happy times you shared. There are always smells around us; again, our brain logs them and moves on. As writers we use them to our advantage to create an atmosphere or to move a story along.

Sound

When it comes to sound, we can relegate usual sounds to the background and only notice when something out of the ordinary happens. Think about the hum of the refrigerator, the air conditioning, birdsong in the garden. Once we're used to something we don't notice it. But if we are hearing people, our ears filter out much more than we know. We place things in proximity. Is that sound close or far? Should I be concerned? Is the ice cream truck close (for those that remember ice cream trucks!)? We certainly recognize when there is a sudden sound and react accordingly.

The way in which we describe this sense can allow the reader to hear it rather than have the sound explained. This is easier than we think, because every time we read something we bring our experiences to that reading. So, if we as the writer use the right words in the right way, we can invite the reader to associate with a sound and therefore hear it clearly.

Taste

We can eat something without fully noticing how it tastes because it's what we expect. Eat something that is amazing with unexpected tastes and our brain is trying to sort out what's what and how it can get more. Similarly when something tastes off because it's got an added ugh, or it's gone bad. Taste is very sensory. Babies use their mouths to make sense of their world. It's maybe not used as often as the other senses unless you're writing about food – or other good stuff – but it can be useful for stories to add an extra layer to the writing.

Touch

Think about trying on a sweater that's cashmere, or synthetic. The difference it makes to your skin. A stranger brushing up against you and lingering a little too long compared to a lover's touch that is desired but brief. We often use touch in our writing to indicate a mood. Rough grabbing, sweet stroking, and so on. But there are different places we can be aware of touch. Being squashed into the subway train, lying on sand or grass, an item of clothing that is comfortable or offensive.

***

Taking the senses for granted is normal. For example, if we had to notice everything, each time we walked into our room, it would be exhausting. So, our eyes may only notice when something is out of the ordinary or out of place.

When we are writing, sight is words on a page. We need to make those words do the job that our eyes do. We need to invoke the pictures in the reader's mind and although description can do this, using the senses does it in 3D. When we're describing a setting, we need to pick out the things that enhance the story, we don't need to know everything. The reader can fill in the rest from their experience and imagination.

Sometimes, as Black writers, we are expected to be trauma driven, even when working through the senses. But there are plenty of experiences we have in life that are not traumatic. We are often in spaces where we are seen and are able to relax and just be. We are allowed to have complex lives that embrace everything.

There may be that one teacher in school who wore Paco Rabanne and always stood too close to anyone he was talking to. The smell made you nauseous and as you grew up every time you smelt it on a guy in a nightclub or on the bus, you imagined that teacher and his lack of personal space etiquette.

Imagine using a bus route that took you past a biscuit factory. You may have happy memories of when your mum used to go and buy bags of broken biscuits and the time you spent hunting through the bag for your favourites. The crumbs sticking to your fingers and spilling out over the table. The minute you find your favourite and bite into its crumbly texture. Heavenly. But our character may have a different association that brings it into the Black experience. Think about them receiving a text about their cousin from St Lucia who just received her PhD with no corrections. Or their aunty in Nigeria who opened her boutique and made her first million Naira and wanted to let them know as her favourite! Suddenly being on that bus going past the factory and receiving that phone call or message means that smell has moved them into a Black experience. There is an association with the smell of happy times that doesn't just involve enjoying a McVitie's biscuit with tea, but which connects our character to her roots.

Mini exercise

Take notice of where you are.

Look around you. Is everything in place? Is anything missing? Is there anything that isn't normally there?

Have you recently eaten something, drunk a coffee or a juice? Water tastes different depending on the brand or the tap. Do you notice it?

Are there any smells, either pleasant or unpleasant?

What are you sitting on? How does it feel?

Work out what you can hear. You may have to concentrate. Decide whether it's close, short distance or long distance.

Discussion point

- How could using the senses describe a Black experience without relying on stereotypes?

- Do we always have to have food smells, chicken and rice, hair oil, coconut body oil?

There are some products or foods that we can associate with a particular way of being, but there are also other smells and sights that we can associate with a particular time of life.

Example

She's offered another drink that she doesn't mean to accept, but of course she does. She minds the lack of sweetness less this time. She can feel herself loosening up, but she doesn't want to get any looser . . .

The doorbell rings . . . She can hear how her voice changes when she speaks to men. It is softer, and the vowels are more pronounced . . .

Steve is sitting close. He touches her arm every now and then as he makes a point . . .Their feet are resting on a mock-sheepskin rug. She likes the silver lamp that stands in the corner, casting dappled shadows . . .

She . . . sprays the room with perfume from the windowsill. It's heavy and sweet and only marginally better than the smell of sick.

JACQUELINE ROY, *The Gosling Girl* (2022), 20–1

Using the senses in the right ways brings the reader into the story and allows them to experience it in a deeper way. *The Gosling Girl*, by Jackie Roy, allows us to be part of the character's experience and brings in the senses in a natural way that doesn't disrupt the telling of the story. This is an example taken from different parts of the chapter that explores the senses in a way that isn't intrusive in the story. So, it doesn't break up what is happening but flows into it. Notice how she integrates the senses into the scenes, allowing the reader to experience them. We are not reading a list of senses but are engaged with the telling of what is happening.

Exercise 1

Imagine you are on the beach, or in a school building or a high street. Using the five senses, write down the experience of being there. This is more than a simple description. You are experiencing being in the space. But you can only use sight once. There are several ways this can be done. We can be with you emotionally, maybe you're thinking about something that is going on in your life, or something that you are looking forward to. Or you stand in the space and close your eyes and experience it in that way. Rely on the other senses to describe the space, let them naturally tell us what is going on and to draw us into the telling.

Exercise 2

Close your eyes and imagine being somewhere you have been before. It could be a previous home you lived in, the school or church you went to when you were growing up, your favourite aunty's house.

What can you hear? Is there a particular smell you associate with the space? Can you describe the smell in words? Imagine touching something there; what does it feel like? Do you associate a taste with that space? Perhaps you were eating something when you were there one time. Finally, consider what you can see. All the details. In your mind, look around slowly, pick out the things you normally take for granted because they should be there.

Now write a description, using all the senses you've just considered. You will find that you add much more detail than if you were actually in the space. This is because we layer the space with the several experiences we've had of being there. We remember people, smells, articles from different times and bring them into the memory, forging it into one description. This is a good thing!

This is how the senses create setting as an additional character in our stories.

Round up

The senses are an integral part of our writing. We don't use them all the time for everything: that would be exhausting to read, just as it would be exhausting for our brain to acknowledge everything all the time. We use the senses in our descriptions when they will enhance the story. They need to add to the experience of our character rather than be there because we think they should be.

Think about the senses and which ones would enhance the writing. Be aware of how often you use sight. Sound and smell can introduce a character just as well as their eyes or clothes.

Read

Take note of where the senses are used and how they work within the following short story, 'Underground', by Courttia Newland.

Look at the two opening lines and think back to chapter 1. Why do you think he has started the story this way? What is he trying to convey?

The following sentence is an example of using the sense of touch without specifying that touch is being used: 'The knees of my jeans became saturated with fallen rain . . .' We understand because we know how something feels when it is saturated, especially when it is an item of clothing on our bodies.

Pick out the sentences that use the senses. Ask yourself if they are integrated into the story or if they stand out. Look at how the senses are used and think about how you can use them in your own writing.

'Underground'

Courttia Newland

She was staring. At me. Hands clasped tightly together, head tilted to one side, forehead carved with the slight hint of a frown. Her face thin and pale with cold, her eyes wide and circular. I tried to keep my mind on what I was doing, why I was there, but it was almost as though, with my gaze cast at the flowers and stone and the tangled grass that sprung from damp earth, I could feel the tug of some invisible force wrench at me until my eyes were lifting, raising my head, finding her again. Then I would experience a sharp pain in my gut – nerves or something similar – and I would grow hot, embarrassed, like a child caught in the act of performing some wrong. My head would fall, my gaze return to the trinity of objects beneath my feet, knowing she had seen me noticing her.

I knelt in the grass hoping that would obscure me from her vision. Or her from mine. The knees of my jeans became saturated with fallen rain, but I didn't care. I bent my head and began to pray, murmuring beneath my breath, closing my eyes and picturing my mother, wherever she may have been. Time passed. I opened my eyes, face-to-face with the inscription etched into black-and-grey speckled stone: *In Loving Memory of Altina Solomon: Mother, Sister and, most of all, friend – 1952–2004.* There was more to say about my mother, had my family or I possessed the money to say it. Funerals were costly things, headstones and inscriptions even more so. A broken pillar or down-turned torch, like some of the older gravestones, might have symbolised what she meant with greater clarity, yet that single-sentence epitaph was all we could afford.

I got to my feet, wiping stray grass from my knees and there she was. Fingers overlapping, dark eyes unblinking, staring at my face. A shard of my former tension ran through me, and then I felt outrage, anger for having been disturbed. I stepped towards the woman, trampling long grass flat beneath my heavy boots. I felt my hands form fists by my thighs.

Her fingers unravelled, leapt towards her face. Covered her mouth in shock. She stepped backwards, away from me. A small noise escaped her lips, a sharp note that floated across the space between us, although I heard the sound in my mind, rather than my ears. The woman's eyes grew larger, darker as I watched, stunned and unable to fathom what was happening. They stopped me in my tracks, while everything around me – the grass, the gravestones, the looming trunks of trees overhead – seemed to fall away into nothing.

The dark shadows cast by leaves were gone. White light reflected from cloud-filled skies bathed us in sunshine. Behind the woman, a group of men wearing flat caps, shirts and britches were standing beside a deep pit, leaning on spades, talking. Beside the pit were a number of plain-wood coffins, stacked on top of one another like logs for the fire. Thrown, I looked around, breaking my stare from the blackened expanse of the woman's eyes. In the distance, though I wasn't quite sure at the time, I swore I could see the faint outline of a horse and carriage.

Then we were back beneath the shadow of leafy trees, my head reeling and the thump of a migraine beating at my temples. I slipped on wet grass, almost falling onto the stone, and when I looked up she was still watching, her dark eyes slightly less fearful. I was on my knees again, my hands buried in long grass, propping myself up, breathing heavy. I heard the rustle of her approach, and for a long while I could not bear to look up. It was only when I noticed the damp hem of her dress, the frayed tan material and tightly stitched lighter patches, that I realised how out of place her clothing was. Mouth open, I looked the woman up and down, partly hoping she was an illusion conjured by my own isolated, crazed mind.

It was a simple dress, a one-piece garment that fell past her ankles, although I could see a white petticoat beneath. The sleeves reached as far as her elbows and the neckline was low, slightly exposing a full cleavage. The front of her dress was criss-crossed with black ribbon. she wore a white piece of cloth to cover her head, with another black ribbon wrapped around it to keep the cloth in place. I'd seen enough history books to recognise that this woman, and her clothing, were not of our time. I remembered the men's flat caps and britches, the rhythmic sound of horse hooves. A shiver exploded throughout my entire body.

The strangely dressed woman was standing over me. Her curious frown returned. She peered at my trembling body as though I'd asked a question in a foreign language. I tried to breathe more fluidly, and stumbled to my feet, the world tumbling and turning around me. Once I was standing and looking into her face, I found myself drawn in by those amazing eyes, so black they seemed like large pupils. I could see my own face reflected back at me. I couldn't move. A hand caressed my cheek. Her fingers were as cold as the gravestones that sprouted from the earth, but I didn't have the power to flinch, even if I wanted to.

Ashampo?

She had spoken, but once again the sound avoided my ears. The strange, although familiar word occurred in my head like a thought I had formed myself. Still, the voice was not mine.

John?

This time I was surer that she was speaking to me, and the question in her eyes was obvious. I shook my head, looking away at a dusty cemetery worker strolling along the pathway where moments ago I had seen the illusion of a horse and carriage. The worker ignored us both, whistling as he walked by. She turned my head with a cold, gentle finger, until I was looking at her again.

Yes. You are John. You recognise me no longer?

I wasn't sure how to respond. I could only stare into that reflective darkness, my mind reverberating *No, No, No,* until I realised my answer was not sufficient. I steeled my thoughts and forced myself to focus on each individual word.

I am not John. My name is Joshua.

She smiled suddenly, severe expression breaking like an explosion of birds taking flight. She looked young and beautiful and her dark eyes sparkled.

It has been too long. You have forgotten. I forgive you.

Then she was tugging my hand with frozen fingers, leading me from my mother's gravestone, across the grass and onto the rain-soaked path with no idea where I was being taken, only that I should follow without protest. Something in her eyes, her manner, her *being* told me I could trust her. It sounds ludicrous, but I can't say any more than that.

We walked hand-in-hand amongst the forest of stone, the overhanging branches of ancient trees and the heavy silence of the cemetery, without another word, spoken or otherwise. Past lofty mausoleums tinted green with moss and crawling weeds. Between all manner of grieving angels, their wings spread ready to take flight, or folded neatly behind them with a finger pointed upwards, indicating where the escaped spirit may have fled. I gripped the cold fingers and let myself be led. I saw a handful of people on that short walk; none recognised the woman, or even noticed she was there.

We reached a lonely place that seemed quieter than my mother's burial site, which was not far from the Garden of Remembrance on the cemetery's west side. Here, there were leaning headstones, grass and weeds as high as the average man's waist, a crumbling Colonnade. It was a large, dilapidated building that stood on a slight incline, thick stone columns erected every five feet. I imagined it might have been grand and spectacular decades ago, but those glory days had long faded. Beyond the cemetery walls, the rear windows of a huge building I happened to know was a youth hostel overlooked the grounds. Not far from where we were walking, the Colonnades' only keeper, a rusty black and orange cat, sat curled on a gravestone. It squinted at my companion and yawned.

We trampled through tall grass, over the tombs of the dead until we had climbed onto the raised concrete of the Colonnade. Here, the woman left me to bend before a trio of flagstones, looking as though she might attempt to shift them with her bare hands. I approached to help, only for her to wave me away. I stood to one side, reading inscriptions on the weathered memorial tablets, listening to the drip of water on stone. When I looked again, she'd lifted every one of the flagstones herself. beneath her feet there was a dark window of nothingness that almost seemed solid. The woman grabbed my hand, tugged me towards the window. I pulled back, my hypnotic spell broken, realising what she wanted. When I shook my head as violently as she had moments before, she smiled again, took my face in both hands, pushed hers close until I could feel light breath against my nose and lips. It was as cold as the touch of her fingers, and smelt like a cool breeze. It was soothing. I closed my eyes.

Home, I heard inside my head, as she turned to look at the black window, indicating the rusting spiral stairs that led below. This time, when she tugged at my hand, I offered no resistance.

It was as dark as death itself in the depths of what I realised was a catacomb, and yet I found I could see. The air was stale and unused, and smelt of damp wood, although I breathed easily. Water dripped from the roof. I could hear the scratch and squeak of unseen animals. Coffins were embedded in the walls behind rusting steel-fenced compartments, though I turned my head, not wanting to dwell on the sight. My hand gripped in her ice-cold fingers; she took me deeper into the catacomb, which was as large as a church hall, into a room where there were no coffins, only a simple low-slung iron bed, a gas lamp, an elaborate wooden desk and mirror, a wardrobe with open warped doors and no clothes. In the centre of the small room more flagstones had been removed. There was a hole, the bone-white remains of a fire. The woman guided me to the bed, where I sat, looking at my sparse surroundings. It was a dank and hellish place and I had no fear, but I also had no idea why I was there.

She stood before me, staring with those topaz eyes. It was embarrassing, but there was nowhere else to look. Her thin face was earnest, and although she was too dishevelled and shrouded by pain to be beautiful, her looks remained bewitching. I had a sense that had she been alive in any real sense of the word, the pumping of her heart would have brought colour to her features that would attract any man, in any time. The woman's eyes filled with tears. I felt a hot burn in my cheeks as I realised she might well have heard my thoughts. I reached a hand towards her, which she took and placed on her cold cheek, her chest. As I had guessed, her heart was still.

Ruth, I heard. *They called me Ruth*.

I nodded to show I understood. She released my hand and pointed at me.

John. Yes?

I had no more idea whether I was really that person than she it seemed, but I had decided I would accept it as fact, as I had accepted everything else. Ruth smiled, then without another word crossed both hands, clasped the shoulders of her tattered brown dress, and pulled it from her body.

Beneath the clothing, she was naked. Her dark body shone, though I couldn't tell where the light came from. As she turned to hang the dress in her wooden wardrobe, I caught sight of long, angry scars across her back, running from shoulder to hip; so many that they overlapped over and over, deep weals in her flesh that would never heal. The wounds reminded me of torn brown paper. I couldn't help myself; by the time she was facing me, my eyes had already leaked tears onto my jeans. Ruth stepped towards the bed, sat beside me, cradled my head in her hands. She rocked me as though I had been the victim, back and forth, and although in some way I knew I was, I couldn't quite work out how. I caressed her in return, fingers skimming dry, untended skin. On her shoulder I found the brand, a blackened, raised portion of flesh bearing two letters, **RC**. Without knowing whether she would allow such a thing I found myself kissing Ruth on that scarred flesh, hoping to soothe her pain with my lips, erase what I'd found.

The dreams, when they came, were terrifying. I saw Ruth at work in the fields, sweating beneath a windward sun only to look up and turn her body to receive the lash of a whip from a red-faced man on horseback. Blood seeping through thin clothing like an ink stain. I saw her asleep in a meagre hut, light from the full moon as the hut door opened, a shadowed figure that crawled onto her body and held her mouth closed with a rough hand as she fought and kicked. Some nights there was childbirth, a cane-coloured baby snatched as soon as the umbilical was severed, Ruth knocking at the back door of the big house only to be turned away by an elderly African with sorrowful blue eyes. I felt her misery as she stood in a row of captives by a dockside and opened her mouth so a young blonde man, too hot in his foreign attire, could inspect her teeth.

After four nights the dreams were of a crossing, chained within the bowels of the ship, rocking against Africans from tribes she could not understand, speaking several broken European languages. Shivering as she stood on a London dock and then a huge wooden stage in the city centre before hundreds of well-dressed buyers and sellers, chained with her countrymen and women as a barker with a long stick pointed. Ruth being taken away on the back of horse-drawn cart to a mansion house in the centre of a large field, where there were others dressed in clothes that had once been fine. I felt Ruth's cautious delight when she came into the kitchen, scrubbed and ready to work, only to notice a man that could have been my twin – John – already smiling.

At first, I was so overwhelmed by the visions I could barely ask questions. I had become a creature of nocturnal habits, resting during daylight, climbing the spiral stairs to breathe fresh air at night. Ruth produced food from somewhere; vegetables and meats she'd heat on the tiny fire in her darkened room, sometimes even fresh fruit. I sat on the cold flagstones of the Colonnade waiting for her to cook our meal, for it was too smoky for me in the catacombs. When she came topside with tin plates and cutlery in hand, we would eat and look over the still grounds of the cemetery. I felt serene, at home for the first time in my life, for I was not a man comfortable with the world in which I lived. I guessed I wasn't the only one. Others roamed amongst the crowded headstones at night. I could hear low voices, the rustle of movement too loud for any animal, sometimes even the light of a match or torch. Ruth seemed unphased by our nocturnal neighbours. I tried to relax and force myself to feel the same.

One night, sitting outside in the dark after dinner, there was that strange flash in my head, the heavy thump at my temples and blurred vision. When I blinked it was suddenly daylight. The cemetery was transformed. The marble stones and columns of the Colonnade were gleaming, the weeds and long grass gone. The horses and carriages were back, but this time many of them dotted the landscape. There were far less trees, which provided an unobscured expanse of low-cut grass, the sporadic white of tombstones and rich farmland beyond the cemetery walls. I could see family groups in Victorian clothing, the men in top hats and tails, the women in elaborately tailored dresses with dainty umbrellas in hand. They walked the pathways, inspecting gravestones and memorial tablets with great interest.

The thump in my head became a migraine. Soon, the world grew dark again. When I came to, I was back inside the stifled depths of the catacomb, lying on the tiny iron bed. Once again, I had to marvel at Ruth's strength. I winced from pain, watching her watch me. I remembered my first vision, of men in flat caps standing by the crumbling hole of a mass grave, leaning on shovels.

How did I die?

Ruth turned away.

Please. I must know.

Still she would not turn towards me, even as she spoke.

The doctor could not say. He thought it may have been your heart, but he was not sure. I could not afford the best.

I lay back, silent.

One day you were alive, the next they put you in the ground. When it was my time, I returned. I do not know why.

I sat up and held her hand. She was shaking.

Don't question what has happened. It could leave you, I told her. She faced me, a tiny smile on her lips, stroking my cheek.

You always used such wise words. That is what I missed most.

We hugged then, her icy body tight against mine.

Now there were two within the catacombs, it was only a matter of time before we were discovered. By the sixth night I noticed voices and torchlight drawing close. When I looked at Ruth she said nothing, but I could see the glow of the yellow beams reflected in her dark eyes. She shuffled, uncomfortable as the voices got louder and when I tried to ask whether we were in danger she only shook her head and looked away. For the next two days I waited for my dreams to tell me what might happen next. Although they were silent, I knew our time in the Colonnade was short.

We hadn't been sleeping long, wrapped amongst one another like the weeds that embraced tombstones, when I heard the static scrape of flagstones above. I jumped awake, as I had been on the edge of slumber, only to see that Ruth had already raised her head, listening. She put a finger to her frosted lips, grabbed my hand and led me from her tiny room. As we were on the far side of the Colonnade and our visitors were moving by torchlight, it would take them time to reach our room. Ducking so the wild, jerking beams wouldn't catch us, we moved quickly towards the far end of the catacombs where I could already see another spiralling set of stairs. Ruth climbed first, letting go of my hand to push at the flagstones. I looked across the huge, dark space, watching silhouettes inspect the incarcerated coffins and grunt at each other, then inexplicably begin to smash and tear at the wood. Ruth gave a huge grunt, struggling with the flagstone above her; when it toppled aside with a crash, the torch beams froze, flew erratically, pointed at the stairs, at us. Moonlight spot lit our position. Cool air caressed my upturned face. Before I could fully appreciate that fact, there were shouts and running footsteps. I felt a cold grip on my hand and I was wrenched upwards, feet clattering on rusty iron.

Topside, Ruth tugged me up to join her one-handed, easily. It was the first time I had witnessed just how strong she was, though I barely had time to take it in. She was pushing me from the Colonnade, ordering me to run into the long grass before she took off herself, gathering her undergarments in a fist. The sharp edges of tombstones scraped at my heels, yet I hardly felt them. The voices of the men stirred me on and I followed Ruth to the nearest path where the going was easier and the soles of our bare feet rang out in harsh explosions that filled the night. She seemed unsure where to head, so I pumped my legs harder and took the lead. I'm not sure how long we were chased, as my noisy heart drowned their progress, but I found a place where the cemetery walls had crumbled and were undergoing repair. We climbed fallen brick and stone until we reached the other side, stumbling onto Harrow Road. There, we paused, I with my hands on my knees panting hard, Ruth straight as a ruler, chest hardly moving, as though she'd taken a midnight stroll. It took a moment longer for me to catch my breath; when I did, it was to witness the crazed look of wonder in Ruth's eyes as she tracked cars, vans and buses, reflected by drivers' faces as they craned their necks to see what the hell we might be doing on the Harrow Road, half-naked in the early morning. Crack heads was their summation, no doubt.

There was nowhere else to go but my flat, a one-bedroom housing association residence not far from Kensal Green station. Ruth was silent all the way, gazing at the world around her. Over a few hundred yards our roles were reversed. When a dog barked, she clutched my elbow; when a motorbike roared, she nearly set off running again. I spent the entire walk crooning beneath my breath, holding her by the arm, telling her we were all right now.

I'd left my keys in the catacomb, though I was pretty absentminded and always kept a spare under a neighbour's plant pot in our shared front garden. When we entered the flat, feet kicking at the mound of letters, it all seemed too much for Ruth to take. She fell against me, superhuman strength gone, and I had to fairly carry her up the stairs to my front door. Once inside, she lurched from room to room like a blind person in new surroundings, fingers splayed, touching everything. She caressed the television like a long-lost family member. Jumped when I lit the gas cooker. Gazed at my Blacksploitation poster of Pam Greer with a look of confusion, made a similar expression when she found my PC. When I switched on the television she screamed as though she had seen an apparition, backed away until she fell onto my sofa, and wouldn't move. She stayed there for the next half hour, sometimes getting up and touching the screen, the rest of the time sitting on the sofa and laughing. She only looked at me once, with the expression of a child given a new toy; after that I was ignored. I didn't mind. It gave me the mental space to look through my letters, become reacquainted with my living space. I walked into my neat, well-ordered bedroom and sat on my bed, deep in thought.

I had never lived with anyone besides my mother. Since she died there had only been my aunt, who lived in Watford and I saw on rare occasions. I'd studied nineteenth-century literature in hope of becoming proficient, but jobs in academia were rare, and other, more dynamic tutors had taken the posts, I guessed. I worked part-time in the local library and claimed housing benefit to take up the financial slack. I'd always been a bit of a loner, made precious few friends. Now I had invited a woman who most accurately could be described as a spectre to live with me. The possibility of a negative outcome was overwhelming.

I set about my room, getting rid of anything Ruth might somehow deem offensive; the scant collection of girlie magazines I'd bought and instantly regretted; a hip-hop CD my aunt had given me; a copy of Joseph Conrad's *Heart of Darkness*. When I was satisfied everything was in order, I squared my shoulders and took a deep breath until my chest was full. I exhaled and left the room to offer Ruth a cup of tea.

3

Creating authentic Black settings

- How do we use setting as part of the story?

- Black spaces: to decode or not to decode, that is the question.

- Setting as emotional space.

Setting influences writing and the impact it can have on the story almost acts like another character. This chapter will discuss what and how we reveal where a story takes place. There are Black spaces that we may or may not decide to decode for our readers. Consideration will be given to the setting as an emotional space, in addition to physical. We will consider how we show this and what techniques we can use. There are different ways to situate our writing and characters that give all the information we need about the subject we are writing about. The language we choose can indicate the way the writing will be received.

The way we use setting in our stories makes a difference. It sets the tone. It tells the reader what is happening emotionally to our characters, what is likely to happen in the plot, whether it's a light or dark story, happy or sad, scary or fun. It adds to so many dimensions. If you think about a movie or a TV show, the same space can be welcoming and open one minute and then change to something dark and threatening the next.

Let's imagine walking into the kitchen and opening the fridge as a normal everyday thing that people do. You take something out, put it on the counter, chat away to the kids or partner. The sun is shining, you're all happy and planning out your day. The next time you go to the fridge, the house is empty. It's midnight. You open the fridge door, and the light throws everything into shadow in the kitchen. You shake your head because you got goosebumps. You take out the slice of cake that's been calling your name since dinner time. When you go to close the door, you notice that something is out of place with the fridge magnets, but you can't work out what it is. The sudden dark as you close the door makes you catch your breath. You imagine you have seen something move outside the window. The same space, a different feeling. Of course, in movies we get dramatic music and lighting to help set the scene but in writing we must do that work on the page with our words.

There are many ways in which setting can move the story along or ask the reader to pause for a moment to reflect. But always the setting should be working for the story. When we think about a Black setting, we must consider what would make it 'Black'. We have the obvious stereotypes of gang houses and alleys; guns and drugs; churches; prisons; aunty's house with doilies and 70s wallpaper and a drinks cabinet housing the best sherry glasses that are being saved for visitors who never come.

That is too easy. It follows the Western idea that Black people and therefore Black characters can only occupy certain spaces. In our writing, we get to challenge that notion. We get to place our characters in any space where people might be. We don't have to make our characters stand out or force them to fit into any space. We get to treat our characters as central to the story. No apologies or excuses needed. But how does that make a space a Black space? It is about who our character is in that space. It's about allowing them to just be, whilst creating a setting that speaks to the story we are telling.

One of the important rules about setting is that you don't spend time describing something that has no bearing on the story you're telling. For example, your character may walk into a room. You then go on to describe everything in that room and spend a lot of time going over every detail. All the while your character is standing there doing nothing, probably looking at their nails or staring at the ceiling waiting for you to get on with it. Now, if you are describing the room because your character is taking note because they're going to have to use something in that space that moves the story along, well fair enough, go for it. But don't let it stop the story. And don't spend time on something that will not be referred to again. We don't need to know every ornament on the shelving unit unless those ornaments are going to be used in some way. We only describe what moves the story along.

So, our character may stride through the room, trip over the rug that's seen better days, bump their knee on the dusty coffee table, swear and knock over the vase that belonged to Great Aunt Clementine. All of this could be part of the plot or show us who the character is. We get the idea that the room is a bit shabby from the rug and the dusty table. It's probably quite cramped too if our character can't walk through without bumping into things. Our readers can fill in the blanks of what the room is like and later on in the story we'll find out the significance of Great Aunt Clementine's vase.

Discussion point

- How can we use setting to move a story forward?

- What are some of the things a good setting needs?

- How can we make the setting part of the story?

- Do we need to describe all the details of a space?

- Where will using the senses help?

What are the things that are important about setting? We can take the ideas from real life. Think about all the places you know; think about anything you've read or seen in movies. What can you recall about the setting that enhances the scene or the story? Read something you've written and ask yourself the questions about what the setting is doing. Is it adding to the tone of the story? Does is evoke some emotion? Does it reveal something about the character or the plot?

Example 1

Whenever I think of my mother, I picture a queen-sized bed with her lying in it, a practiced stillness filling the room. For months on end, she colonized that bed like a virus, the first time when I was a child and then again when I was a graduate student. The first time I was sent to Ghana to wait her out.

YAA GYASI, Transcendent Kingdom (2020), 3

This is a very simple setting and yet it manages to convey a lot of information. Even before we get to the final line and the word Ghana, we understand that the narrator sees this as a Black space, with the word 'colonized' being used to describe her mother's actions.

Although we are not given an enormous amount of detail about the room, we can picture it. I imagine the heavy curtains drawn closed. Maybe there is a sliver in between where they don't quite meet and the sun pierces through and slices across the room. Dust motes are falling around the bed. Because the stillness fills the room, I imagine it feeling warm and smelling 'beddy'. I can see discarded cups and glasses on a bedside table that has an old-fashioned lamp on it. There is an absence of sound and the soundlessness fills the protagonist's ears. Discarded magazines or books, plates, notebooks, all of these would be scattered around the bed around the mother-shaped lump under the covers. None of this is written but this is what a good setting will do for the reader.

Example 2

Amma
is walking along the promenade of the waterway that bisects her city, a few early morning barges cruise slowly by
to her left is the nautical-themed footbridge with its deck-like walkway and sailing mast pylons
to her right is the bend in the river as it heads east past Waterloo Bridge towards the dome of St Paul's
she feels the sun begin to rise, the air still breezy before the city clogs up with heat and fumes
a violinist plays something suitably uplifting further along the promenade
Amma's play, The Last Amazon of Dahomey, opens at the National tonight

BERNADINE EVARISTO, Girl, Woman, Other (2019), 1

This is the opening chapter of *Girl, Woman, Other* by Bernadine Evaristo. She captures the mood of the character. The languid motion of the barges, bridge and river show movement, the weather is light not oppressive, uplifting music along the promenade – again movement and then we find out the protagonist's play is opening, so she's happy and feels as though things are moving forward. Once more a Black space is created through the name of the play that is opening at the National – Dahomey (modern day Benin) and the use of the word Amazon.

This example takes us into the emotional setting of the character as well as the physical setting. It incorporates the senses as discussed in chapter 2 and takes us on a journey with the character. It places us very much in one space – London via Waterloo Bridge and St Paul's Cathedral dome – whilst also taking us into Africa through the title of Amma's play.

Exercise 1

For this exercise, think less about the story for a moment and concentrate on creating a believable setting that draws the reader in. Don't forget to use sentence length and structure and the senses to complement the setting.

- Create a setting to reflect a story idea. This idea can be around the plot or the character, the mood or the circumstance.

- Is there a very ordinary space that can tie the setting to the story? It could be a school, an office, a town centre, a house.

- Whatever is in the space will be relevant to the story arc. Which means we don't add articles to a space and describe them unless they are useful and will be used.

- Thinking about what we did in the previous chapter with the senses, how will you decide which senses need to be used in a setting?

- What if the space/setting is emotional rather than a physical space, how do we show that?

- What if the setting is a memory? How do the senses/emotions work with that?

Exercise 2

For this exercise, I'd like you to look at the opening scene of a movie. I recommend *Far From Heaven* and it's available on YouTube, simply look up the opening scene to *Far From Heaven*. I like to use this opening because it gives us so much information about what we are about to watch. We know the era the movie is set in; it opens with beautiful autumnal trees but as the camera pans towards the town we see something different that gives a foreboding. Lots of little clues that everything is not idyllic.

Imagine this is the opening to your story. Describe it as fully as possible, thinking about the music, what you can see and using a hefty dose of imagination.

Round up

Setting can be physical or emotional. It is an integral part of the story you are telling and should be used as such. Only describe what is relevant to the story. Think about what will be used in the story and what the reader can fill in with their own imagination.

Our Black characters do not have to move through stereotypical places and as long as the setting fits with the story, it's the correct setting for your character.

Read

The following short story uses setting to complement the story. You'll notice there are no long descriptions; I mainly use the descriptions to enhance the emotions of the main protagonist. Meisha is conflicted, the setting is a tangle of mangrove roots, barnacles, brackish water and disappointment. It's a Black space because it's in Trinidad in the Caribbean and my characters are Black. And in case there was any doubt: 'the red mangrove with its roots hanging down like well-behaved dreadlocks'. Our character automatically associates the mangrove tree with her own point of reference – dreadlocks.

Identify the sentences that refer to setting as you read the story. Look at how setting is a natural part of the story and see how you can incorporate this type of setting in your own writing.

'Waiting'

Muli Amaye

It started with love. That's where it always starts. Meisha knew that, but it didn't help. Sitting next to him on the green flat-bottomed boat, she wished love didn't exist. That it couldn't trap you with strangers, slowly chugging through a swamp.

He had insisted on the trip that day. It was on his Trip Advisor list of 'must do' things in Trinidad & Tobago. It had been the first place she had wanted to take him on when he arrived. Her favourite. She'd raved about the spectacular show produced each evening, about how it was different every time she went. She'd booked it twice before she realized it wasn't going to happen. That her clear enjoyment of Caroni was enough for him to move from the 'yeah, yeah, let's do it' in front of her friends, to the mocking eye roll when she mentioned it over dinner, just the two of them.

She hadn't suggested it that day, remembered not to ask, allowed it to be his idea and feigned disinterest. But he was leaving soon and the shiver that danced along her limbs like spider crabs running up the mangrove roots grew stronger each day. Meisha couldn't tell if it was fear or excitement, but it didn't matter which, the result was the same.

They had pulled up into the car park for Nanan's Tours, and Meisha wondered how she would manage in the slow boat with him beside her. She'd felt his eyes and the curl of his mouth, the disgust. Before leaving the car she sprayed insect repellent on her arms and feet and offered it to him, not making eye contact. Of course, he didn't need any and flung the door open with fake choking noises, as though she'd tried to poison him. Avoiding muddy puddles, she'd led him over to the waiting area. The smell of tomcat and wet fur was strong following the recent downpour. He'd worn his white Converse. She'd suggested he put on his black ones as they were leaving, before she could stop herself. He hadn't even answered her. Now she could sense the accusations hitting her in the back, stinging with their sharpness.

She looked around and saw the place through his eyes. A dirty riverbank, dogs and cats harassing visitors and staff alike. She asked him to pose next to the Nanan's Tour sign and before he could refuse an older lady, American, stepped in and took the phone. 'Go on', she said, 'let's have one of you together.' He turned on his charm and the sweet smile that had ruled Meisha's life since forever. Drooping his arm over her shoulders she felt the weight of his twenty-six years seep into her bones. The woman handed back the phone, reached up and patted him on the cheek, as though he was a small child, not a grown man. Meisha smiled, relaxed a little.

Sitting in the corner on the ply board seat she hoped the flaking green paint wouldn't stain her jeans. He was still chatting with the American, a returnee, who lived in Florida and extolled the virtues of the man-made rivers and swamps there that were so clean and open. Normally, there were plenty plastic bags adorning the riverbank but she only saw a solitary empty pack of Dunhill cigarettes, upended in the mud next to a freshly blown sweet packet. The mud gave up an unsavoury aroma each time there was a gust of wind. She tried to be bothered by it but failed. Glancing up she watched for any sparrows flying in or out of the nests that were wired into the roof. Dry twigs occasionally caught in the breeze and fluttered down, dancing with the lone dragonfly that seemed trapped even though there were no walls. Meisha took in the jumble of seat slatted green boats facing every which way.

This was just the way it was. And she realized that whenever she talked about the Caroni Tour it was only the end she thought about. She accepted the two hours meandering the swamp to get there. Enjoyed the meditative journey, depending on who was on the boat because some people couldn't quite get nature and insisted on laughing and joking throughout.

One of the boats belched out smoke and the smell of the diesel was nauseating. She hoped they wouldn't be in that one, even more so when she saw the guide using a plastic bucket to remove water. Not when there was a new looking Yamaha 50 High Thrust engine attached to another boat. It was stealthy and quiet and didn't have fumes. Another guide was brushing along the seats with a cocoyea broom looking as though he was getting it ready. Her shoulders relaxed a little more, one less thing for him to complain about. Normally when she came it was the older engines that were used, but there had been an article in the paper about thefts. People coming in the middle of the night to help themselves. New engines were bought and removed with the painful old winch each evening. Driven away to be kept under lock and key and camera. Beside her he was getting restless. She could feel it, even though he was still chatting away to his new friends. Finally, they were called forward, boat with new engine held steady with rope, hands offered, feet on seat and then sitting. Waiting.

Before they even reached the old cement dam he was fidgeting beside her. Clearly bored and unable to walk away unless he wanted to wade through three feet of dirty water and scramble through the red mangrove with its roots hanging down like well-behaved dreadlocks. Meisha tried to shift slightly away from his body, listened to the guide who was pointing out tiny fiddler crabs scurrying down holes in the mud. The bigger blue crabs were less timid but still shied away and one passenger loudly explained to his wife that they lived in the larger holes. The guide's green laser light kept missing them and passengers on their first visit showed displeasure at not seeing anything but holes in mud and then a collective oooh when they finally noticed one. He sighed loudly. Saying a million things that only she heard.

Meisha closed her eyes and bit back regrets she wasn't ready to acknowledge. It hadn't always been that way with him. She had tried so hard when he was young. Fought with anyone who dared to question what she was doing or how she was doing it. He was hers. She'd only ever wanted the best for him. To shield him from the ugliness of the world. Her ribs ached with the memories. His sweetness and curiosity had always enthralled her. He was so bright, so enquiring. Others didn't have the same patience to deal with it, but she never tired of answering his questions. Of helping him to learn in his own way, at his own pace.

The guide stopped the boat and pulled in under the mangrove. Insisted on silence while he searched the tops of the trees, looking for two tawny screech owls that had been spotted nesting there the previous day. Apparently, it was very rare to see them together and especially in the daytime. Next to her he was muttering in the back of his throat. A deep guttural sound she hated. The owls were spotted high up and shielded by mangrove leaves, an appropriate number of photographs taken on mobile phones, though Meisha knew from experience few would come out well. The owls blended so easily with the branches the majority of the tourists wouldn't know what they were looking at when they reviewed their pictures.

The sun was beginning to dip as they moved along. A snakeskin was spotted above them, drawing gasps from someone in the back. The tree boas when seen knotted up sleeping amongst the leaves, brought screeches from some. Meisha closed her eyes. She knew they weren't going to bother them, or drop on their heads, or drip venom. It was all part of the tour. Her chest began to burn and she tasted the sourness of stomach acid that was stirred into action. He was still now, and it was worse than when he was fidgeting. She hardly dared to breathe.

She had read all the literature when he was growing up. Believed that freedom was all that was needed to grow a healthy human. The system was against them, wanted to create drones, drive the creativity from anyone who showed a spark of originality. She hadn't wanted that for her boy. Didn't want him to always be the one that was told what to do by adults, wanted autonomy for him. Children needed space to be, not boundaries to block them. *She felt a stinging slap in her right cheek.*

Slowly, slowly they chugged along the channel, Meisha listened to the guide as though she hadn't heard it before. Brackish water, a mixture of salt and fresh. She wondered if fresh tears were always salty or perhaps they, too, were brackish. By the time they reached the canopy of shade she was damp, her backside, the bar across her back, where her body contacted others, felt sticky and she welcomed the mangroves that offered protection. Passengers were getting louder, excited. A tri-colour egret made a show of gliding along in front of the boat. Cameras clicked, people stood up, heads hit mangrove roots. Meisha enjoyed the bird's effortless show, envied its freedom. His head was turned looking at trees, totally disinterested. The guide pointed to the side and pulled the boat closer to the bank. There was a termite nest clinging to a tree like a small bear sleeping. Next to her he muttered an expletive.

The boat turned left down the North–South channel. A green and white sign attached high up in the tree advised that entry was by permit only. A pied water-tyrant landed on a branch right next to the boat. So small and pretty with its black and white feathers, Meisha thought about the name. She couldn't imagine something that cute could be tyrannical.

The passengers around them grew louder. There was disbelief that the barnacle looking things on the mangrove roots were oysters. They looked like they belonged on the bottom of ships, though the guide assured anyone who wanted to try that they were mini aphrodisiacs. In front, a woman shouted instructions to duck as they passed below some low branches. She felt him stir beside her and glanced his way. There was a girl, a young woman, in front of them, Meisha hadn't noticed her before, but clearly, he had. Her stomach clenched and she crouched over, arms wrapped around herself.

His first girlfriend had looked at him in the same way this girl was. They'd been sixteen, getting ready for prom. He'd been in school for three years even though Meisha hadn't wanted him to go. Had wanted him to learn only the things he cared about, but he'd insisted. She'd made the mistake of telling him about his father. Tried to impress on him that education doesn't mean learning and that he knew so much more. But he'd fought with her, insisted she enrolled him in a school, that she did the right thing for once. Meisha circled her temples to ease the pain that was ever present. His father only believed in education; she'd shielded him all those years for nothing. She only wanted what was best for him. He'd come home from the prom early. Refused to talk to her and never saw his girlfriend again. That was the last time she'd met one of his partners until Alice.

By the time they reached the open lake and the sun was grasping at the tree tops, he was chatting to the girl who was blushing and clearly charmed. And he was good looking, Meisha knew that, people had commented on it his whole life. His beautiful skin tone, neat, short dreadlocks, hazel eyes, generous mouth that was capable of smiling and laughing and spitting vileness. Meisha caught herself. Shook her head. It was nothing. He was leaving. Soon. And at least he was happier now. That's all she wanted. For him to be happy.

Slipping through the channel into the wide, open lake, mud flats were evidence of the low tide. The guide made a joke about the boat getting stuck and people getting out to push. Meisha had heard it before. What she hadn't seen before, though, were the flamingos that were wading through the mud. They were so close she felt she could reach out and touch them. Taking out her phone she leaned past him to take a picture. He looked at her as though she'd walked into his room without knocking. She sat back. Tension ran across her shoulders and up her neck.

The boat pulled up opposite the island where the show was about to take place. The Scarlet Ibis. National Bird. So bold in colour, so sure of where they were going, and when they landed on the trees the island looked like a giant poinsettia. Even he had to be impressed with it. The guide slung the rope around a branch sticking out of the water. He began telling them about the national bird. Each visit Meisha gathered a little more information. She could easily read up on it, but she liked to be there, to listen and absorb while she watched the show unfold. Two flamingos flew overhead and the camera shutters worked overtime, everyone trying for the perfect shot. Beside her, he was mocking the tour, its slowness, the birds that were just birds and nothing to be excited about. And that young woman was giggling and agreeing with him. Boldly staring into his eyes, sure of what was about to unfold for them.

Meisha looked out beyond the island. There were grey sheets of rain like galvanize over the northern range that looked as if they were moving towards them. The passengers were growing restless. They'd been sitting for five minutes and not one single Scarlet Ibis had shown itself. The white egrets were coming in low, barely skimming the water and disappearing inside the trees, out of sight, safe. The flamingos were moving to the far end of the lake, getting ready to roost for the night. A small group of Carib Grackles circled above their heads, black and shiny, looking like miniature crows. Meisha shuddered.

The clouds were gathering and anxiety was crawling through her entire being. She ached from her hair follicles to her toenails. He was relaxed now, charming and affable, flashing his smile. The way he turned his head allowed the setting sun to bathe him in red tones, drawing out his beauty, the part of him that Meisha knew was there. She surreptitiously took a picture of him. It felt like they were sitting in two different worlds. The rain threatening with dark clouds on one side and the sun setting on the other. The young woman was smitten, taking out her phone, giving her number, making plans for the weekend that could include him, if he wanted.

There was something gnawing at Meisha, something she had to do. She had known when he called and said he was coming to see her that something wasn't right. He'd feigned concern for her saying that he wanted to check that she was doing ok. She'd expected Alice to be with him, but he was alone. Unhappy. Moody. Meisha hadn't asked what was going on. Hadn't wanted to know. He was her boy. She was his mother. Of course, he would come to her if he was sad.

Suddenly the dark grey clouds split open and a tiny slice of rainbow appeared in the sky. It was so unexpected, so vibrant and bright. Meisha seemed to be the only one to notice it as the tourists grumbled about the foreboding rain and the fact that the show had not begun. As though the guide could direct nature to do what they wanted, what they expected. Meisha held up her phone and snapped a picture of the rainbow. As she lowered it her finger hovered over the WhatsApp icon.

Alice had sent her a long message with details Meisha didn't want to know, so she had ignored it. Had argued with herself about these young women that made up stories when they didn't get what they wanted. Then counter argued about Alice and how decent she was and how she didn't have any reason to lie. Watching him start again there, in her place, with her sitting right next to him, Meisha felt like scales had been scraped from her eyes. Calmness came up from inside of her, a lightness that was normally reserved for watching thousands of Scarlet Ibis alight over the island.

She opened that message again, sitting there in Caroni, and knew what she had to do. As the engine purred into life and spots of rain reached them, she began typing. The grumbles of the tourists at not seeing a single Scarlet Ibis rang in her ears. All that waiting for nothing. The journey back was so much quicker. Nothing to stop and look at, chasing the last of the day's light. Bats with triangular wings dipping amongst the mangrove, swooping down to the water then disappearing into the roots. Meisha had to wait until they reached the broken-down dam where the fresh and salty waters met before she had a signal on her phone. She hesitated. He was her boy. What if . . .? She felt sick at what she had to do. Eyes brimming, she looked out over the swampy undergrowth at the border of pink Poui trees that stood out against the dark northern range. Closing her eyes, she pressed send.

He'll arrive back next Wednesday morning, British Airways. Do what you must. I'm sorry.

4

Fully functional Black characterization

- How to create authentic characters.
- Understanding how experiences affect characters.
- Allowing characters to be three dimensional.

This chapter will discuss how we collect information about the different characters we create and how to keep them authentic and three-dimensional. We, as fiction writers, need to know our characters completely. It is only in this knowing that we can produce the necessary reactions to situations we place them in. In order to understand what we are writing, we need to know the characters involved. That isn't to say that all the information we know about a character ends up on the page. It's enough that we know why they do what they do, feel what they feel and can justify their reactions if asked. It's not enough to just say, that's how she/he/they are. This is especially important for Black characters in ensuring that they are not othered. Our characters are often the driving force in our stories. They want something, or something has happened to them, or they've done something. We need to know our characters fully. We need to understand how they act in certain situations and what it is that has made them react in the ways that they do.

Characters that we write will always be a composite of people we know or have come across in some way. And more often than not there will be aspects of ourselves in there, even if it's our shadow self that we don't acknowledge. Have you ever read something really gripping with a terrible character, written by the sweetest person you could hope to come across? I have and I'm surprised each and every time. Early in my writing career I may have thought that the character was a reflection of the writer, and I have definitely had people assume that I am my characters and what happens to them happened to me.

When I was researching for my novel, I interviewed older Afro Caribbean and African women. I walked around the area my novel was going to be set. I read about the era it was to be set in, studied everything I could on the 5th Pan African Congress and checked which women would have been there. I thought about my elderly character constantly, and when I began to write her, I knew who she was. I knew her so thoroughly that when I talked about the story to people who grew up in the area, they would ask what her name was because their mother might know her from back when. She didn't exist except on the pages of my book. She was a composite of all the women I had interviewed, all the books I had read, and my own grandmother. By knowing this much about her, I was able to create a real character that resonated with readers, someone that even I believe could have existed in Manchester in 1945. I knew her so well I was able to create a background for her, a whole life in Nigeria with a cousin, a wicked aunty and a strong stubborn streak that put her in the situation she ended up in.

We have our characters, and we have our stories. Often Black characters have been on the periphery of stories. They have been written out of having autonomy. Sitting quietly on the margins and allowing life to happen to them. This is not only the case with mainstream stories, but we ourselves have failed to develop our characters fully. Almost as though we are afraid to stamp them across the page in all their glory. Partly because it is not expected and partly because stereotypes are what sell books. But we are allowed to have Black characters in full colour and 3D who do the things that every other character is allowed to do. We can have characters who have a bad streak in them, because that's an imitation of life. All humans are multifaceted and cannot be all good or all bad. Our characters can be instigators and not simply victims of life.

There can be an element of disbelief from publishers and teachers who see Black characters (and Black people) as one-dimensional. They believe the caricatures that are displayed in movies: that Black people/characters can only be one thing, although there can be exceptions if it's only one or two. It is our job as Black writers to portray our characters and ourselves as complex as any other character. Those of us who are diasporic writers can write a white character perfectly, because we have to know who they are in order to survive. We need to write ourselves with the same confidence. We have to acknowledge our completeness on the page.

Discussion point

- What do we need to know in order to produce fully rounded characters?

- Is it enough that characters move from point A to point B and react as they do?

- How do we produce fully functional, fully rounded, believable characters who work for us and our stories?

The following are examples of what I think are good characters. That is, they are characters I could believe exist outside of the pages of a book or a story with all the foibles and flaws that make someone interesting.

Example 1

How was I to know he had a bad heart? All I wanted was to dance one more time in my life. I heard the music playing in his room that was right across from mine and something came over me, a joyous feeling that I had had in my life only once before, so I went over and asked him to dance. What's so wrong with that? It's true he had just moved in and we hadn't been properly introduced. But I didn't 'drag him around and assault him and cause him to freak out and have an attack', as Matron told Celia in this overly dramatic mimsey-mamsey way of hers, all hands and eyebrows and jangling earrings and shoulders working.

She believed it, of course. Not that she said anything, in that lawyer-ish way of hers. Nothing showing on her face. I sat there like a school girl in Matron's most uncomfortable chair trying to look comfortable. My arms and legs crossed. I didn't say a word. I never do. One thing I've learnt in life is to hold my tongue. Which is why She knows nothing. Though O how I cringe every time that scene pops up before my eyes, the most embarrassing moment of my life, a moment – I might add – totally and absolutely out of character. I truly, truly do not know what made me do it, me, the shyest person on earth. But how will they know that, since I have no intention of confessing?

OLIVE SENIOR, *Dancing Lessons* (2014), 1

Example 2

Omar sat, uncomfortable, in the front seat of the maxi-taxi minivan. His lanky frame was hunched and contorted, his face puffed-up like a country crapaud. He was pissed. He'd been pissed when he left his mother's house in the quiet, turtle-watching village of Matura about an hour ago, and he was pissed now as the maxi neared the bustling hub of Pleasantview Junction. He didn't want to be back in Pleasantview – but his mother, Josephine, wouldn't listen. He didn't want to return to the tiny, suffocating room with the chicken-wire window where he rented from the Jagroops. He didn't want to spend another day of his life bagging groceries at the Save-U Supermarket. And to make matters worse, he didn't want the old, fragile picture frame in his duffel bag – but, this morning, Josephine had made him take it anyway.

CELESTE MOHAMMED, *Pleasantview* (2021), 37

Example 3

It's the summer. You start to think about your chakras.

You are committed to becoming your best self. You are not going to care that everyone else is getting married or getting promoted, or having babies or buying houses. When friends tell you their good news, you will simply smile and then send them gift baskets of baked goods because your heart is a lighthouse, as opposed to say, a Black dwarf star, colder than Alaska.

You make an action plan and you post it on this blog, for the sake of accountability. You have precisely ten followers, so if you mess it all up, hardly anyone will know.

KAREN ONOJAIFE, 'Here be Monsters', in *Closure* (2015), 29

Three examples from three very different stories. I have purposely used different points of view to highlight that our characters don't need to be written in first-person for us to know them. Read each one of the examples and see what you can glean about each of the characters. What do you know about them? What can you fill in that isn't being told? Use your experience of people that you know, of stories you have read and movies you've seen.

How do we create our characters? Often we just write and they develop on the page. We do it without thinking and they may turn out okay. There are different ways to develop our characters. But for the purpose of understanding how we do what we do, it's a good exercise to develop a character from scratch.

There are many elements that define us as people, and these elements can be attributed to our characters. For example:

- Childhood illness

- Friends

- Escapades

- Absent/present parents

- Trips

- Movies

- Foods

- Firsts

This is a very simple list, and there are many more items that could be listed, but each of these elements, along with our personality, would develop us in a particular way. Imagine a child who has a long illness and must spend weeks in bed or in the hospital. It will shape a part of them maybe in the fact that they missed out on things their siblings did or they couldn't go to school and were behind their peers.

They could have been seriously ill and the fear from their carer would stay with them even if they weren't aware of how serious the situation was. This will play out when they come up against a situation that is similar when they are older, and which triggers them to act in a particular way. If we are to develop fully rounded characters, we need to understand them. This can come after the fact. For example, you write a story and you know it's good and the character is believable; at the editing stage you can then consider the things that have made your character who they are.

Now it's time to create a character and put them in a situation, knowing all that we know about them.

Exercise 1

- Create a character profile.

- Start with the list above.

- What things have happened to them in their life and when?

- Who were they close to and who did they hate and why?

- What are their accomplishments, hopes and dreams?

- Personal attributes: what are their worst/best features?

- Add simple information such as appearance, age, etc.

Exercise 2

- Place your character in a situation.

- Imagine they are trapped in a lift in between floors. How do they react? How do they get out?

- Write a couple of paragraphs as though it is the middle of a story (or the beginning or the end!)

- Don't forget sentence length for effect; the senses to bring us into the situation; the setting, so we know where it is happening. Create tension.

- Justify to yourself how your character reacts from the list of attributes you gave them earlier.

Round up

Characters need to be three-dimensional. We need to know who our characters are in order to know how they will react in a given situation. We develop our characters as composites of all the people we know, books we've read and movies we've seen. And there are elements of ourselves in each character.

We must make sure our characters take up space on the page. They don't have to apologise for being there and they don't need to live in the margins.

Read

The following story, 'The Water Beneath My Feet' by June Aming, has a complex and complete character. Read the story carefully and see what information you can glean from it.

Who is Kira? What are the things that have shaped who she is? What makes her a fully rounded character?

There are tells throughout the story: the way her parents act, the things her grandmother says, the missing brother.

Try using some similar techniques when writing your character.

'The Water Beneath My Feet'

June Aming

'To understand another person,
You must swim in the same waters
That drowned them.'

No one ever talked about Michael.

I knew what he looked like from the wrinkled pictures I had found tucked inside an accordion folder that my father had labelled 'things'. I was most interested in the one of him on a bicycle racing across the dirt road with the bushes as his backdrop. His pant legs were torn away like vagrant couture showing bony knees poised in mid-air about to bare down against gravity. His hair raced with the wind as it trailed away from his face, his eyes were trained on something in front of him. He seemed oblivious of the camera aimed at him, unintentional slight to the one who desired to capture this moment of flight. I looked with intent at the picture of his face to see his eyes and whether he could be sending a message to me, the sister that he would never meet. The picture was so faded that it was hard to make out the tint of his eyes, or the hue of his complexion. When I turned it over, someone had scribbled 'Michael, son. 1995–2008'.

I couldn't tell if we were the same, or different. I did know, though, that he was silence on the tongues of my parents while my name,

Kira, was a shriek through the house when dinner time came around. And he was dead but I . . . was . . . alive.

'Kira, you was up late last night?' Ma looked at me out of the corner of her eyes, like she already knew the answer and she was waiting to see if I was lying.

'No.' I lied anyway, concentrating on scooping up the watery tomato choka with a piece of dosti roti. Pa and Ma were eagerly mopping the plate like the experts they were, fingers stuck together like human spoons.

When the meal was over, as usual I wheeled Nan out of her room and placed her at the table for my mother to feed her. Nan, my father's mother, had lost her eyesight but doesn't know it. Or pretends to not know. Nan would sit on the front porch commenting on the day like an astute weather woman. On a hot day, when rays of sun bathed her exposed arms and legs she would smile and announce that it would be a beautiful day and ask us if we didn't see the green leaves of the frangipani plant with its crisp white flowers at the top like a Sunday hat. Ma would mamaguy her and agree that it looked beautiful. I wanted to ask her how she knew that it was in bloom if she supposedly couldn't see but the cut eye that slashed in my direction from my Ma's deep brown eyes always gave me pause.

After dinner, my parents left to run errands leaving me to keep an eye out for Nan.

We sat in silence, and I could feel myself dozing off.

'I could see you crying you know, Michael.' My eyes snapped open, and I stared at Nan. She was gazing into the distance through gray, milky pupils, her face contorted, her lips turned down and quivering. I moved closer to her and stared at her intently.

'Nan?' My voice joined the chorus of cicadas in the yard, raised an octave higher by the surprise of the comment.

'Michael, I tell you not to go that day. I tell you not to go. Give she some time. You is a good boy so just give she some time.' Nan was insistent. Her eyebrows were two caterpillars crawling across her forehead, her head shaking from side to side.

'You know Michael?' I asked her softly. I was an intruder on her path of sorrow, but it was the first time that anyone except for my curious wonder had uttered that name.

'Who is Michael?' Her sadness morphed into shock and the caterpillars raised their shackles.

'Michael. My brother. The one who died before I was born.' I needed to know more, and I was not going to let her abandon me on this maiden voyage.

'Kira, I don't know what tricks you are up to but if you come up with anymore stupidness about imaginary boys I will tell your Pa.' Nan was in full grandmother mode now and I wasn't sure if to get her back in stream with the 'Michael' talk or to change the topic before the Pa thing stuck in her brain and regurgitated itself as soon as he walked through the door. I decided to get her into her bed and revisit this on another day. This conversation was not over.

Fingers crossed, Nan seemed to have forgotten the incident and I waited for another opportunity. Ma, of course, was suspicious when I asked if I could take Nan for a little walk.

'Maybe I shouldn't look a gift horse in the mouth. Wheel Nan to the back of the yard where she like to feel the river breeze. Be careful though, the rainy season here with a vengeance and the backyard a little muddy. Try not to get the wheels stick up in the mud and for God's sake, don't let the chair turn over and Nan end up in the mud.'

It had been a tricky route to navigate but I chose a stop at the furthest end of the yard by green fig trees where they were spreading their expansive leaves high and wide providing the perfect shade from the two o'clock sun. As I stood behind her, I tried to think of ways to steer the conversation back in the direction of Michael.

'Nan, you had a lot of brothers and sisters. What do you think about me being an only child? Not even a brother to talk to.' I waited. She was silent for a while, and then her eye lids fluttered a bit and she smiled.

'Hmmm. Brother? You don't have a brother?'

'Do I?'

'No. And you damn lucky. Them boys used to get licks for so. Except for the green-eyed boy, Michael. No one could beat Michael. Nothing that happened could have been his fault.' I threw a gaze over my shoulder to make sure that Ma was far from ear shot. Here we go.

'What do you mean, Nan?'

'I mean your Pa ain't carry your Ma twenty-four hours through the marriage threshold when this woman come knocking, knocking on the front door. When it open braps, she shove the boy into the house and tell your Pa that is time to mine his own child. Well girl, yuh Ma almost pass out. This big boy, twelve years old was a grandchild I never know exist. And your Ma? Worst yet. She pack up all she clothes and get ready to leave if he didn't get rid of the boy.' I was breathing softly because I didn't want to break the spell.

'But the boy mother, that woman who face look like it mash up with hard time and hurt, done gone. And the boy stand up looking scared. I stay quiet, quiet and I wait. At the end of the day that situation was between husband and wife. They talk from then through the night. I give the boy some bread and tea and I send him to sleep in the spare bedroom. The room you sleeping in now. Anyway, sun turn to moon and back to sun and the boy live with them for a year. Until he dead.'

'I know he drowned. I saw a piece of paper clipping from the Express newspaper in Pa's things. How did he drown?'

'Who?'

'Michael.'

'Who name Michael?'

From then I found myself always staring at my father. Who was this man who had married a woman without telling her that he had a child? And who lets their child drown? Would he let me drown? Would he put me on a bicycle, take a few snap shots with a camera and then send me to the river to drown?

Nan's story felt like I had taken a step into another dimension. I just couldn't shake this need to find out more about Michael and I knew that Nan was the only link. I found myself trying to give her memory a little jolt. Once when she was sitting in her own world, smiling at her own thoughts I snuck up behind her and whispered his name in her ear. Nan was startled and almost fell out of her chair. Ma asked me if I was trying to kill Nan by sneaking up on her and I almost blurted out that I was trying to unkill my brother.

My answer came one night in the most peculiar way.

'Bhola,' Nan said this word with such certainty and gusto at the dinner table that we all jumped with surprise. Pa's eyes opened wide like two dosti rotis beginning to rise on the tawah and he began adjusting his eyeglasses as if that would make everything normal again. Ma's eyes were steadied on the plate in front of her.

'Nirmala Bhola. That was she name. Poor beti.' Pa was already rising from his seat ignoring the chair that had fallen to the ground behind him.

'Nan, I think you finish. I think you should go to your bed now.' Pa was pulling her chair backwards while she was eagerly stretching her hand into her plate.

'But I not done with my food. My belly still hungry!' The plate came crashing to the ground; potato, rice and channa, a hot, muddy paste splashing across the floor. As Pa forced her from the chair and onto the waiting wheelchair, her body flailed around like a freshly caught carite. Ma's wide eyes were glistening. Pa tilted the chair upwards and wheeled Nan crazily into her room before shutting the door behind him.

As soon as I was allowed computer time I typed the name in the filter, and I saw the full news story. Thirteen-year-old Michael Bhola had decided to skip school and go to the Ocino River with his friends. According to witnesses, he entered the water headfirst. All the boys thought Michael was joking when he remained underwater, but after several minutes passed and he didn't rise to the surface they jumped in after him. One of the boys said that they just couldn't get his body to the surface. His head was stuck in the mud at the bottom of the river. His father had said that he was a good boy but since coming to live with him Michael couldn't seem to catch himself. His mother could not be reached for a comment.

The next day I wheeled my bicycle out of the front yard. Ma had just started filing Nan's toes and she was confident that her perfect daughter was inside her edge of tomorrow room studying for end of term tests and Pa had gone into town. I was going to be the silenced child today. I was going to meet Michael.

I pressed my foot on the peddle against gravity and felt myself surging forward along the gravel road that had led my brother to his death almost twelve years earlier. I tried to imagine what our lives would have been like if not for the turn of a single event. Would he sit with me and go over my schoolwork, or would he be the one who grabbed my hand and took me on a school day escapade to Movie Town? Would we spend hours in exhaustive fervour as we told jokes together and drove Ma and Pa crazy with secret handshakes and knowing nods?

I raced as fast as my thoughts, my home funnelling like a tornado into a dot behind me. The Ocino River breeze was opening a chasm that seemed to magnetically pull me through. It took me five minutes to get to the track that led to the river. I got off my bicycle, held the silver handlebars and guided the wheels across the pasty, uneven earth. My knees were knocking together, shaking with a mixture of excitement and uncertainty. I didn't know how I was going to meet Michael.

I looked at the descendants of the trees and plants that must have scraped Michael's arms as he made this same journey. The foliage that lined the track grew rich and lush with the recent rains while the clumps of log orchids splashed its white, yellow and lilac across the greenery. I listened to the distinct sound of the corn bird whose ancestors must have witnessed the plunging of a boy to the depths of a river. That sweet chirp that was present for both the beginning and the end of a life.

A panic rose from my belly into my throat and was beating under my tongue. I steadied myself, thought of Michael and moved to the bank of the river.

The murky water smelled of dead fish and rotting fruit and islands of debris flowed slowly by. Mounds of soggy takeout containers and plastic drink bottles. Some of the bottles, both water and soft drink, were crushed and twisted in someone's attempt to be 'green'. As they floated by, they shone like diamonds under the glint of the sun, but I wasn't fooled. I knew they were all heading to destinations unknown; either out into the wide, ceaseless ocean or to be forever trapped in the crevices of the rocks in the Ocino River. As I walked along the riverbank, my rubber slippers slapping out of the gluey mud with each step, I finally reached a spot where the river deepened and formed a small pool. This was where I imagined my brother would have gone for his afternoon dip. I passed my foot across the surface of the flowing water that was not glimmering as I thought rivers should. A glance upward told me that the sudden gray skies held no mirror to the watery bed, and I knew that if I was going to wrap myself in the waters of my brother that I better do it then.

I entered the river like a cutlass slicing through the tip of a coconut shell. The biting water bubbled and broke against my ankles, singing the sweetest of lullabies. The soft mud of the bed rose between my toes and cradled my feet as the sound of the wind through the leaves and the rush of the water calmed my pounding heart. With my legs descending into the dense darkness of the river I moved towards the center of the pool, my dress rising to the surface and dancing around my waist. I was a lily, a beautiful flower growing wild in the Ocino River.

As thunder slammed against the sky, a light rain started to drizzle, and I knew it was time to leave. It was time to say goodbye to Michael. I moved my body forward, but the mud embraced my feet tightly and I couldn't move. The more I tried to pull against it the tighter the grip and I felt myself being sucked in by the sludge and water. The rain began falling steadily and the movement of the current became more intense against my ankles. I wiped my eyes with the backs of my hands, aware that my feet were cemented to the ground and the water surging forward was forcing my chest to collapse into the running river. As I fell face down, I pushed my hands in front of me to brace myself. My fingers became fused with the mud and on all fours, I was like a dog in a storm. I held my breath and felt my lungs burning as oxygen tried to make its natural escape through my nostrils.

As I surrendered to my fate, I could feel the stones at my hands and feet swirling around, fossil bones clawing at my skin, working to free me from the snare. I opened my eyes and peered into the concoction of weed and mud that moved around me, a whirlpool of light green iridescent tears that loosened my body and pushed it back up to the surface of the cresting foam. I was shoved onto the rocks that scraped and sliced my skin. I climbed out soaked and shaking, pulled off stray reeds that adorned my head like a wreath, gripped the bicycle handle with prune-fingers and made my way back out.

I heard the clanking of pots in the kitchen as I snuck around the back of the house and tried to get to my bedroom through the side door. As I slipped through the door frame I came face to face with Nan, sitting in her wheelchair smiling at some memory or some imaginary scene playing before her. I stood there silently in the puddle at my feet. She turned towards me, the smile disappearing from her face.

'You see Michael?' The question was a whisper. I walked towards her, a trail of loose reeds, mud and river across the floor. She reached out to me, and I placed my palm in her hand. Her lips quivered and pursed as she bent her head forward and kissed my wet hand. She took the shawl off her shoulders and handed it to me.

'Clean up the floor before your Ma come in and your Pa get home, then go and take a bath, Kira.' She settled back, and the smile reappeared.

As I stood in front of the shower stall still wet and cold like a rain-soaked dog, for the first time in a long time, I felt strangely clean.

5

Black voices

This is a small chapter that builds on characterization. We will consider authentic voice and how this is presented on the page and explore what needs to be taken into consideration. For example: what's the character's socioeconomic status; their educational level; where were they brought up; their history; what time period are they in; parents' background, and so on. We must feel them and understand their opinions, prejudices, likes and dislikes, which is where our character profile comes in.

One of the ways we can get stuck when we are writing is when we make each character voice a reflection of ourselves, our opinions and our likes and dislikes. Each character will have their own way of expressing. Think about your friend group or your family. There will be specific words or phrases that are used by different individuals. There will be a tone and an inflection that you would recognize because that's how your aunty speaks, as though she's quarrelling all the time, or your best friend always has a smile in their voice when they're telling you something.

Have a listen to the people around you. Try to recognize their patterns of speech. The specific words they use, how they use them. Listen to the inflection in their voice; you've probably never noticed it before, because that's just how they talk. Now, I'm not saying you should point out to people what they say and how they say it; this is just for your own research purposes! We don't always listen to ourselves either. I was working in a university with a Greek linguist. She came to me one day and said she knows which students are in my classes because they would answer questions with 'I reckon it's like this or that.' I had no idea what she was talking about. I reckoned she was making it up. But she wasn't. It was a phrase I used often, without thinking about it. The students who had English as a second or third language had picked up on it and started using it (in the correct context I might add).

Just as we talk in particular ways, there are distinct voices in our writing. Our own voice as author will always come through the writing. We have turns of phrase or particular grammar 'tics' that will identify our writing. This means that we don't have to worry too much, but it's important that we distinguish between ourselves and our characters. An example I like to give for this is Murakami books. I went through a phrase of reading a lot of them, one after the other. What I started to notice was that although the mood in each book was different, there was a distinctive tone to the narration and that it was slightly dry and sardonic. Although each character would sound different, there was a similarity about the general tone which was how I could identify a Murakami book without seeing the name of the author on the cover.

Discussion point

- What is noticeable about your voice?

- Do you use specific phrases or words?

- Can you identify someone's voice on the page?

Exercise 1– write as though no one is reading!

- Write a short blog about something that bothers you.

- Write it clearly as though you are journaling.

- It could be anything: dog owners not cleaning up after their own dog, traffic, people who don't queue, whatever got on your last nerve this morning.

- Write it out, really vent about it. Nobody is going to read it, this is just for you, so you can really let loose.

- Don't think about grammar and the correct way to say something – just write.

- Think about what makes this your voice – particular words or phrases or thought patterns.

We'll be coming back to this exercise in a little while and I hope it was therapeutic to write out that niggle! But first we're going to consider character voice and how this differs to our own voice in our writing.

Character voice is very important in fiction writing. We cannot have every character speaking the same, using the same intonations and not varying at all. We don't have to worry about our own voice because it will come through naturally. It's important to stay true to the character. This is why we have to know our character through and through.

Think about a character you have created. What's their socioeconomic status? What is their educational level? Where were they brought up? What's their history? What time period are they in?

Answers will tell you the voice of your character. We must feel them and understand their opinions, prejudices, likes and dislikes. Through the character's voice we get to see who they are and why. Look at the following examples and pick out information about the characters. You will notice that the first two are in colloquial language and the rules are exactly the same. If our characters speak in standard English or a local dialect, we stay true to who they are, and everything we know about them will dictate their voice and the language they use.

Example 1

This morning, Papa call me inside the parlour.

He was sitting inside the sofa with no cushion and looking me. Papa have this way of looking me one kind. As if he wants to be flogging me for no reason, as if I am carrying shit inside my cheeks and when I open mouth to talk, the whole place be smelling of it.

'Sah?' I say, kneeling down and putting my hand in my back. 'you call me?'

'Come close,' Papa say.

I know he want to tell me something bad. I can see it inside his eyes; his eyesballs have the dull of a brown stone that been sitting inside hot sun for too long. He have the same eyes when he was telling me, three years ago, that I must stop my educations . . . I tell you true, the day I stop school and the day my mama was dead is the worst day of my life.

ABI DARÉ, *The Girl with the Louding Voice* (2020), 1

Example 2

Oho. Like it starting, oui? Don't be frightened, sweetness; is for the best. I go be with you the whole time. Trust me and let me distract you a little bit with one anasi story:

It had a woman, you see, a strong, hard-back woman with skin like cocoa-tea. She two foot-them tough from hiking through the diable bush, the devil bush on the prison planet of New Half-Way Tree. When she walk, she foot strike the hard earth bup! like breadfruit dropping to the ground. She two arms hard with muscle from all the years of hacking paths through the diable bush on New Half-Way Tree. Even she hair itself rough and wiry; long Black knotty locks springing from she scalp and corkscrewing all the way down she back. She name Tan-Tan, and New Half-Way Tree she planet.

NALO HOPKINSON, *Midnight Robber* (2000), 1

Example 3

I didn't jump on the next flight like someone with nothing better to do, like someone who's kind of been waiting for a phone call like this her entire life. Instead I continued grading my students' papers, which ended up not really being essays but fragmented reactions to a piece of literature we had chosen to read. I had given them a choice between the school's limited options – William Goldberg's Lord of the Flies or Albert Camus's The Stranger – and being strangers themselves, both to English and to Brooklyn, and also because it was a shorter book, most of them voted for the English translation of L'Étranger.

'WHAT?' began one boy's reaction paper. 'I don't thank I be so kalm if my moms dyed.'

Before the phone rang, I had scribbled 'AMEN BROTHER!' in red pencil, in the margin of his single-spaced, handwritten stream-of-consciousness masterpiece. But after hanging up with my father's wife, I wrote him a long note scolding him for oversimplifying and being careless with his spelling. Then I gave him a C.

EDWIDGE DANTICAT, 'In the Old Days', in
Everything Inside (2020), 43

Really concentrate on the voice of the examples you've just read. Work out how much information you have about the character from their voice. For example, in the first example, I see a young girl, she has a faded dress and her hair is a slightly untidy short afro. She's skinny and has an anxious face. None of this was in the piece, but I used my imagination and my experience of being in Nigeria and youngsters that I saw both within my family and outside. I see a version of me. Had the writing been flat and reported rather than alive with the tone and verve of the character, I wouldn't have imagined her in that way.

Exercise 2

- We're going back to our blog of annoying things exercise.

- Rewrite your short blog in your character's voice.

- What changes must be made?

- Does the language and syntax change dramatically?

- Your character has different concerns than you and therefore a different focus on the subject matter.

Round up

Writers have their own unique voice. Character voice is different and depends on who that character is and where they are coming from. We don't have to think about author voice when we are writing, but simply ensure that our characters and narrators each have their own distinct voice.

Read

The following short story by Peter Kalu is a great example of using voice within a piece of writing. There are two distinct voices in this story: the character who is narrating and the proof-reader who clearly does not love his job! Although both character voices have humour in them, they are very different.

What can you pick out from the voices that tells you something about the character? How does the voice of each add to the story? Also make a note of the setting and how it works with the story; look for the senses and see how they bring the character and the story to life.

'Getting Home:
A Black Urban Myth
(The Proofreader's Sigh)'

Peter Kalu

Strange things happen after midnight. Three weeks ago, a Friday, I was coming back from London. Earlier trains had been cancelled and I was in this crowded last train. We were all crammed, my mouth was dry as feathers, my stomach twisted with hunger. I got out at Manchester Piccadilly, uncreased myself, and headed to the city centre bus stop on Oldham Rd[1] to get back to Oldham where I live.

OK, nobody rushes to get back to Oldham. There are no flowing cornfields, no marble terrazza[2] leading to sublime waterfalls in which bronze demi-gods frolic, no sumptuous hot sand beaches up which fishermen haul their boats, land and fry their catch to the praise songs of waiting villagers. Nevertheless, it is home; there is a lockable door there for me and behind that a decent mattress.

I must have dozed on the train like a horse,[3] sleeping on my feet. The train must have been further delayed en route because it was

---

[1] Sic. Fact check: actually Oldham St.

[2] Sic. Cannot mean *terrazza* as in balcony. Probably means *passaggio* (walkway), though these are never marble.

[3] Sic. Generally, horses are not found dozing on trains.

later than I'd thought – late enough for me not to pull out my phone to check the time. Anyway, the battery had no-barred me somewhere between Stoke on Trent and Crewe.[4]

It was late. Late enough for waves of cleaners to be slipping in and out of office blocks. Late enough for McDonalds[5] to have placed a security guard on their door. I get knocked into 'no offence like' by some burly bloke. A girl – a buttery mix of cigarette, alcohol and Chanel No. 5 – ran up and kissed me, no doubt for a dare and I didn't fight it. Someone was dry heaving by the Spar All Night[6] Kiosk. It was that kind of late.

The air was some strange miasma[7] – a balmy cocktail of pepperoni pizza fumes and the convecting heat of a long, hot day was infusing the night with good vibes. Mancunians are not used to this – heat – and they're all a bit thrown. I drag my weary ass through it all, clutching my flight bag of poetry publisher's proofs. As I walk, I reel off a couple of Inshallaahs, God Willings[8] and pluck the entrails of a sacrificial chicken in my sleep-addled mind, before stepping up to the podium, face oiled, every one of my twisted dreads in immaculate place as I ask, please, no more applause, I am not worthy, my poems are not worthy[9]. . .

It was only when I got to the bus stop that I realised it was so late the regular buses had stopped. I looked around. There were six of us huddled there, or spread about, waiting, and only one of us, me, was sober. There is no greater hell than being the only sober person at a bus stop after Friday night's pub and club chuck-out time. Everyone's heaving or bawling or boasting. Nobody but you can read the bus timetable.

I could feel a long line of zeds waiting to rush my brain, I could feel my consciousness slipping off like petals dropping from a fading flower, I could feel the God of Sleep arriving in her spray gold Chariot.[10] A not

---

[4] Sic. No London trains call at both Stoke on Trent and Crewe. Probably means Stafford and Crewe.

[5] Sic. Fact check: there is no McDonald's between Manchester Piccadilly and Oldham Street.

[6] Sic. See note 5. No Spar All Night Kiosk either.

[7] Sic. Miasma is an unpleasant smell. Prob. means ether.

[8] Repetition: Inshallah means God willing.

[9] I am not paid enough to untangle the confusion of tenses in this paragraph.

[10] Sic. Perhaps a reference to the Greek God Hypnos (male). No reference in antiquity to him ever arriving in a gold chariot, whether sprayed, dipped or painted.

unpleasant numbness was just beginning to settle over me when the bus shelter frame shook and the glass I was leaning on shuddered.

This tattooed knucklehead, at least 40, staggers up to me: big chops, red face, rubber legs. He has this wary, 'I'm-a-hard-man-just-finished-my-prison-sentence-for-gbh' look. He sways past me and he's in front of the timetable board thing at the bus stop, squinting.

He turns to me. 'When's the next bus?'

It's a bark, a command. Maybe he's ex-Military, I muse, there were many around now after all the illegal British wars, damaged in mind and body.

'According to the timetable it's at half past 12 – half past midnight,' I say, smiling at him.

'What time is it now?' he snaps back, swaying – which is a hard trick to pull off.

'Yeah, when's it comin?' someone else calls out.

I'm wearing jeans and a Black jacket. I don't have a clip board or walkie talkie or anything, but everyone seems to think I work for the bus company. Maybe it's my rahtid[11] flight bag.[12] My mouth opens to tell them all to go fuck themselves. Then closes again. I shrug off my zeds. The Windrushers[13] arrived in Britain and became bus conductors. Although my roots are African – not West Indian – this subtlety is for another time. I bow to my role. This is honouring our predecessors. We are born to conduct buses.

'It's half past,' I say, 'bus should be along any minute.'

There's a row of three young women, not past twenty, on the doorway steps behind the bus stop. Standing by them are two young lads[14] – the boyfriends I presume, both swaggering drunk, giving mouth[15] to whoever passes by. One of them, the slightly heavier one,

---

[11] Jamaican patois. Yet later narrator says he is of African heritage?

[12] If he slept like a horse, perhaps saddlebag is better here than a flight bag? He has after all stepped off a train, not a plane.

[13] Only reference I can find to Windrushers is to a UK gliding club. Were they blown off course? I suggest cut or rephrase.

[14] Math is not this writer's strong point I suspect. So far seven people 'at or around' bus stop including himself, not six, as stated earlier.

[15] Is this a Northern expression? It reads as slightly sexual, or is that just me? Suggest rephrase or omit.

has a long stick by his side, like a cue stick. A Pakistani looking bloke my age, still in kitchen whites under his coat, comes along. He kind of pauses at the stop, takes in the scene and, wisely perhaps, carries on walking. So, I'm still the only sober guy here. And I'm the only one who's not white, not that anybody's mentioned this so far. I've been around the world; I can handle the situation, I think.

The two boyfriends get a quarrel going with a couple of bouncers standing outside the King's Head just four doorways down. I thought bouncers were trained to be calm and negotiate a situation without violence. These must have been on holiday when they ran that course. The boyfriend with the cue stick that isn't a cue stick starts doing these Bruce Lee kung fu moves, goading the bouncers. His mate is bopping about like the old-style boxers used to. The bouncers are huge. The two lads are puny. Do I intervene? Are you crazy? I decide I can do without the bus, it's only ten miles.[16]

As I walk on there are various yelps, expletives, splintering and ejaculations coming from the vicinity of the nightclub doors. I'm about to turn round but . . . nah, still not worth it. If people's sense of fun extends to rushing at bouncers to get their heads busted, so be it.

I look down the road to Oldham. It's a vast, bleak, empty landscape, known locally as Miles Platting. And now rain.

I suppose in this situation, for some, a hotel becomes a viable option. In my eyes I am a promising young Black poet with several publications under his belt, on the cusp of literary and financial greatness. In the mean eyes of the grasping telephone loan arrangers, I am no more than a 37-year-old Lancastrian with 15 years of sporadic missed payments who, *if I may speak off the record, Sir, you would be best advised to change career. The poetry obviously does not pay; after 15 years even you can do the maths on that one, with respect, Sir.*

Yeah, right. Expensive loans but free careers advice.[17]

So, I'm walking home out of the city centre along Oldham Rd. It's 2am-ish, dark, light rain – par for the course for Manchester. The street is deserted. I walk on and on. The rain keeps it up. A white woman comes into view on the same side of the street.

---

[16] The tenses are all over the place in this paragraph. Again.

[17] Good advice for this writer. Every so often someone at a call centre speaks sense.

The navigation of public space by a lone Black male in the night is problematical with or without hoodies, with or without 'stand-your-ground' laws, with or without a Neighbourhood Watch committee in place or whether or not that space is 'gated' – should we say? Likewise, the ability (as opposed to the right) of a lone woman to move unmolested through the night in whatever kit she's decided to don. I nudge my zeds[18] aside and try to process the information of my eyes. From this distance she could be a very light-skinned Black woman, in which case she might give me a short nod of recognition as we glide past each other, our Black solidarity thing boosted. She is in a party dress. (I would like to provide more information on the dress: e.g. an A line bolero effect with diamante detail and a flounced flapper hemline, scrunched at the midriff, clutched at the waist, and single shoulder strap. But a man's got to know his limitations. It was a dress. A party dress.)[19]

You can speculate why she is walking late at night: A party just finished and no taxi money? A lover's tiff? She's her auntie's main carer and needs to get back to help her auntie dress in the morning? Kids to get to school?

The gap between us is closing and I can see now she is alabaster white. Her body language – a stiffening of the back, a slight drop in the head, a faltering in her footwork – tells me we two are not about to duet to the soundtrack of *Fame*. Her increasing hesitation makes me decide that out of consideration for her, conscious of her vulnerability, and to make it easy for us both, I'll cross to the other side of the street. But she must have had the same idea so just as I cross, she crosses. She's convinced now I'm after her. We're on the same side of the street again and closing. She turns round and starts walking away in the direction she has just come – slowly at first, then faster till she's running. Running away from me along the deserted London Rd.[20] Ah well, I think, I did my best.

It's 2 something am. The light rain has lightened into almost a mist.

Beauty is everywhere, even on the road to Oldham. I come across a scene that slides my eyebrows up my forehead and bunches my

---

[18] Infelicitous?

[19] Should either describe the dress or not. Brackets become annoying. Dress as described is a logical impossibility.

[20] Sic. It was Oldham Rd a couple of paragraphs earlier. Fact check: no London Rd in Manchester leads to or from Oldham.

cheeks. Rabbits. Like a scene out of *Watership Down*, a hundred rabbits are bobbing up and down, nibbling grass on the wide roadside verge where the Italian Restaurant used to be before they flattened it for lack of custom. By day this arterial road roars with lorries, commuters, bankers, fish vans, prison vans, car parts couriers, mobile hairdressers. And lo, by night, there appear jug-eared, white, bob-tailed, jerky-up-and-down, fluffy, cuddly-toyable, cookable rabbits. I've stopped. They look at me. I look at them. They dart, then sit. Dart, then sit. Like my career, or Jockey Wilson[21] (Prince of the Flighted Arrow).

Misty rain is the long-distance walker's dream. This is the mist rain of my high school's feeble showers, the mist rain of a dog's sneeze, the mist rain of a girlfriend's errant hair spray. It soothes the soul and coats my glasses, so I have to keep taking them off and wiping them. It's while doing this that I turn the corner and there's a man, a white man lying on the edge of the pavement. He's shouting, 'Help me! Help me!'

He looks in a bad way. Maybe a car has swiped him. It's wet, late. I'm tired, but you can't walk by. Did not that great Roman thinker, Thucydides[22] say it is the duty of every citizen to come to the aid of his brother? This is the very essence of our civilisation, the foundation stone of citizenship itself, without which the Barbarians will soon be clambering over our city walls, our temples to destroy and we will all be hastened to hell in a handcart? Something like that.

He's seen me coming, and he's been trying, uselessly, to get up. All he needs is a helping hand. I shuffle my flight bag from one shoulder to the other, sweep my dreads off my face, bend down and offer my hand. He sees me close up and a mask of horror has installed itself on his face.

'Somebody else help me! Somebody else help me!' he shouts.

I pull back my hand and straighten up. Some civilisations deserve Barbarians inside their city walls.

This walking home business is not so simple, I decide. Maybe I should try hailing a cab. Three empty taxis have gone past in the last

---

[21] Darts player. Died 2012. Fact check: his nickname was 'Jocky'. Can find no reference to him being 'the prince of the flighted arrow'.

[22] Sic. Thucydides was Greek; need I say more? The entire reference is a load of cobblers, containing as many errors as you can shake a stick at.

half hour of my walking, all of them heading back to the city centre. Surely, they would want to make a little more money before calling it quits for the night? But I've got no cash. There's a Post Office close by with a cash machine in its wall. No one around. No one to panic. I put my card in the machine. A police car screams round the corner.

'Stay right there! Hands where I can see them!'

It's 3 something AM, light rain, dark. I'm tired. 'OK.'

I'm too wet to run anyway.

While they're questioning me – who I am, where I live – a car with no headlights comes screaming round the corner and smacks into a bus stop, concertinas it, then catapults into a lamp post that crashes into the road.[23]

'You going to see to that?' I ask the cops. 'You could do me later?'

They hate advice.

'We're doing fine here,' they say. 'Now, how long have you lived at this address and what is your mother's maiden name?'

They continue frisking me. There's blood oozing from the wrecked car, groans, but they display a complete insouciance to that. Once they've crawled all over me so they can recognise me in the dark by the shape of my frozen genitals, they let me go and proceed to the RTA.

I turn to continue my transaction with the global capitalist system but my card has disappeared. Yeah. Still, the cops who frisked me found a tenner in my back pocket and handed it to me, though they kept my little bag of herbs.

I walk on, watching to hail a cab. For the same reason – known only to God – that buses do this, several come at once. The first has an 'I Heart Pakistan' sticker. It flies right past me – en route to Lahore I suppose. The second cab's driven by a huge Rasta. He appears to be pulling over, then speeds up and off. 'Heh, heh, heh!' Yes, Rasta, you can laugh. The third cab has this bald-headed, olive-skinned guy at the wheel. He veers towards me, only to speed through this mother of a puddle, drenching me. In the back of that third cab I distinctly see the woman who fled back on London Rd and the guy who'd been knocked

---

[23] No local newspaper articles cover this accident and I can find no official crime report on it.

over. The woman is waving my plastic cash card at me. And the guy's waving my little bag of herbs. As I'm taking all this in, the late night bus, all its lights off, flies past me, empty.

The story benefits from ending here.

~~I trudge on. The zeds are swarming the gates of my consciousness, the rabbits are leaping over the walls. A lockable door materialises in front of me. I close it behind me, climb to a mattress and let the zeds flood in.~~[24]

---

[24] Finished? Thank God!

6

Using Black language

- How the use of language enhances a character or a story.

- How to present language on the page.

- To creole or not to creole.

- We will discuss some examples from novels to see how language works.

- Writing in different ways – exercises trying different ways of writing the same thing.

The language we use in our writing does more than tell a story. It provides us with information about when the story is set, where it is set, who is telling us the story and sometimes why. We have to think back to our character profiles and our voice exercises, and we can understand that the language we use affects the story we are telling. We want to go for authenticity, as much as we can, knowing that we write in a different way than live conversations are transmitted.

How can we represent our different characters without falling into stereotypes? This is an important point to consider. We must understand what would make language fit a stereotype. It could be something as simple as a character who is assumed to speak in a particular way because of where they are from. A good example of this came from my research during my PhD. I was watching some old BBC archive material on YouTube about the Nigeria–Biafra war. There were a group of young Nigerians talking to camera; their language was received pronunciation. Not quite the stereotype expected from African peoples in the early 1970s, I'm sure. But why wouldn't they speak in this way? They were academics who were taught under the British educational system by the colonialist. It made perfect sense.

There's also another side to this, though. When I ran some writing shops with Afro Caribbean older people, they were writing stories of arrival, reminiscing on their lives after reaching the UK. One of the ladies asked me to read her work and I did, just as she wrote it. Mainly it was in patois, and I confess, my patois definitely had a Manchester twang to it, but this lady was horrified. In her mind she was writing fully correct standard English, and she couldn't understand why I was reading it like that.

So, we can see that language is sometimes difficult to navigate on the page. But that's all part of the fun of writing . . . maybe. When we create our characters, we know how we want them to talk, whether through narration or dialogue. We are in charge of that aspect of our character, therefore we need to think about how we are depicting that character. This could be because we want to use creole or patois or pidgin, or we want to use slang that connects the character to an era or a place. We must do it consciously and by taking into account who our character is and what we want the reader to hear. It is easy to have all our Black boys talking slang and ghetto, because 'that's what the youth them does do'. But all our characters are individuals, and we have to treat them as such.

Growing up, people could never work out which part of the UK I was from. That I didn't have an accent was the main observation. And that's because I spoke fluid Enid Blyton. I spent every waking moment reading the *Famous Five* or the *Secret Seven* and I lived in those stories. I became a part of them, and that's how I spoke. It was a non-accent that certainly didn't advertise where and how I lived. So as a teenager I taught myself to speak with a proper Manchester accent so that I could fit in. This is just to say that we don't make assumptions about characters and use stereotypes to depict them on the page.

We can certainly use creole for our characters, but we have to be aware of how we are spelling it and whether we are creating something offensive. If the language or dialect our character speaks doesn't have a standardized way of being written, we run the risk of excluding readers from what we write. Simple changes such as dropping a 'g' from a gerund or missing the occasional letter will not necessarily make reading difficult, but we need to think about the effect we want to portray. In my novel, *A House With No Angels*, I chose to have my teenage character, Kutes, narrate without punctuation, in a kind of teenage Skaz as David Lodge terms it:

> For American novelists skaz was an obvious way to free themselves from the inherited literary traditions of England and Europe. The crucial impetus was given by Mark Twain. 'All modern American literature comes from one book by Mark Twain called Huckleberry Finn,' said Ernest Hemingway – an overstatement, but an illuminating one. Twain's masterstroke was to unite a vernacular colloquial style with a naive, immature narrator, an adolescent boy who is wiser than he knows, whose vision of the adult world has a devastating freshness and honesty.
>
> DAVID LODGE, *The Art of Fiction* (2012), 18

I was aware of the difficulties her narration could cause for the reader and kept her chapters under half a page. It was a choice, and I spent a lot of time working on it to get it to the point of legibility.

I advocate for writers using what works for them on the page, but I also think we have to allow the reader to access our stories. Ken Saro-Wiwa with *Sozaboy* and Amos Tutuola with *The Palm-Wine Drunkard* are two examples that show what is possible on the page and still have the text accessible. How we write characters tells a lot about them, whether from dialogue or narration. It's important that we get it right. Choose a way of writing and stick with it. You don't have to necessarily change the spelling of words; maybe try adding a little glitch at the end of sentences, or markers that show the reader it is not standard English. For example, sha!, or eh-eh! Give us clues that we are not reading standard English. Think about how to use the syntax of the sentence without sounding like Yoda!

Discussion point

- Who are our characters and what language would they use?

- To creole or not to creole, that is the question!

- How can we depict a non-standard English on the page?

Example 1

Blind people hear and taste and smell what other people cannot, and what Ma Taffy smells on this early afternoon makes her sit up straight. She smells it high and ripe and stink on the air, like a bright green jackfruit in season being pulled to the rocky ground below. The smell is coming down John Golding Road right alongside the boy-child, something attached to him, like a spirit but not quite. She has been hearing him for a while now – all the sniffling, hiccuping, short-of-breath sounds. But it is not the crying that makes Ma Taffy alert. There is nothing special in this. The old woman is used to the little boy coming from school wet-eyed and vexed with the world for whatever injustice he feels has befallen him this time. 'A backbone,' she often thinks to herself. 'That little boy is in need of a backbone.'

KEI MILLER, Augustown (2016), 5

Although this example is written in what would be termed standard English, the language used identifies it as taking place in the Caribbean. Re-read it and see if you can notice the definitive markers that make this a non-standard English text.

Example 2

Bet-tee! Bet-tee! He didn't need to shout. I was already behind the car opening the trunk to find the lunch cooler. I took it out carefully along with his newspaper and jacket. Sunil stood waiting as I walked past the driver's door. His swift sharp kick in my shin was half expected. Slow coach. You can't come when I call you? What, you ugly and you deaf? Upstairs, I rushed to heat up his food. He was already stinking of rum but the first thing he did was get a fat glass and open a bottle of White Oak. Solo was in front the TV. Eh, boy. Your father reach home and you can't say good evening?

INGRID PERSAUD, Love After Love (2020), 3

I like this example because it mixes languages. We have the standard English of the narration and then dialogue which doesn't have speech marks but is identified by the vernacular it is written in.

Example 3

PEOPLE THINK BLOOD RED, BUT BLOOD DON'T GOT NO COLOUR. Not when blood wash the floor she lying on as she scream for that son of a bitch to come, the lone baby of 1785. Not when the baby wash in crimson and squealing like it just depart heaven to come to hell, another place of red. Not when the midwife know that the mother shed too much blood, and she who don't reach fourteen birthday yet speak curse 'pon the chile and the papa, and then she drop down dead like old horse. Not when blood spurt from the skin, or spring from the axe, the cat-o'-nine, the whip, the cane and the Blackjack and every day in slave life is a day that colour red. It soon come to pass when red no different from white or blue or Black or nothing. Two Black legs spread wide and a mother mouth screaming. A weak womb done kill one life to birth another. A Black baby wiggling in blood on the floor with skin darker than midnight but the greenest eyes anybody ever done see. I goin' call her Lilith. You can call her what they call her.

MARLON JAMES, *The Book of Night Women* (2009), 1

The language used in this example gives us a place and a time. James has chosen to use light patois in this novel. It keeps it accessible but still has the flavour of the language.

Exercise

Write the opening of a story in standard English. Use what we've looked at so far, think about the senses, setting, character, and so on.

Now rewrite it using different characters voices. This will change the language, the tone and the voice. If you need to, you can create a few different characters and try out the voices and the language they would use.

Remember that slang changes with different eras: what was used in the 1980s or the 2000s wouldn't be used now, especially with the advent of cell phones and texting culture. The language we choose can depict an era as well as a social class or country.

Round up

Language is flexible. We use it to the advantage of our story by being aware that it needs to fit with our character, the story being told and the era. Be aware of how it is written on the page: we don't want to be unreadable, so we find different ways of showing if the language is not standard English. We can add 'glitches', use particular words or lightly change spellings. Consistency is key if you choose to write in a creole or vernacular.

Read

The following short story is a fine example of language use. Not only through the words chosen but very much by the syntax of sentences. There is no doubt that this narration is not in standard English, but it is also completely accessible. Spend some time thinking about how language works in this story and how you can use similar methods in your own writing.

'Terre Brulée'

Celeste Mohammed

Boy-chirren different. A daughter will always be yours, but boy-child come like guava: brace yourself; it might have worm. My son, Shiva, was like that; something was eating him from the inside, till he rotten through and through.

But it have good boys. Like this one here, my nephew, Sheldon. We in the gallery, smoking, like how we does every Friday. Me in a plastic chair, Sheldon lolling off on the banister with one hand on the clothesline spanning the gap between this concrete house and the old family house – the wooden one – where he does live with my favourite-sister and she string-band of chirren. Sheldon is the onliest one get me out my room this last month, since Shiva dead. You see, I always had a soft spot for *this* boy. Me, with my whoring, Sheldon, with he dreadlocks and he Black-man father who breed and leave: we is the two outcast in this family. And from small, this boy spirit always match mines more than my own son, Shiva.

Oh Shiva, Shiva! I been crying forty days. And tonight, even though Sheldon and all of St James so excited for Small Hosay parade, I can't celebrate because one thought steady beating me like drum: *Lord, forgive me for Shiva!*

So when Sheldon take a drag on he ganja post, then ask, 'Is how big people could just starve a lil child, ent, Aunty Pinkie?' I mistake it for accusation.

'Catch your damn self, boy. I never starve nobody.'

But he was talking 'bout the Hosay story: 'bout Ali-Asgar, the Prophet great-grandson, and how the infidel-them kill the child during the Battle of Karbala. The story why Muslims does make small tadjahs – baby-size Taj-Mahal-looking tombs – and parade them like funeral through the streets. I did learn that story back when I was a girl in Muslim school, but Sheldon, poor soul, he only now finding out.

'Cease and settle, Aunty. I not accusing you,' he say, sounding real hurt.

I pull on my cigarette, soften my tone, and say, 'I know,' hoping he don't notice how my eye-them full like the barrel catching rainwater to wash he dreads. 'I just saying: *my* child, Shiva, never starve. I wasn't perfect. Me and he father used to war, so I wasn't there all the time, but I always make sure that lil boy never starve for nothing.'

That part true: I used to make grocery, pack cardboard box and tote that bugger up the mountain – me one – to go feed my son.

But it have other parts I can't tell Sheldon: like when I did get lay-off from the Chinee laundry, and I couldn't even pick up a Mister or two to tide me over ('cause I did went with a Vincy sailor-man and catch a bad case of the runnings), so to buy groceries I had-was to pawn my most prize possession, the gold bera bracelet my grandfather make with he own hand and give my father, who then give me. It safe now, under my bed, but to buy it back, I had-was to sex the bowsie-back Mister in the pawnshop. Shiva was worth it to me, though.

Suddenly, the sound of a tassa drum ripple through the night air, like the rifle fire we does hear whenever gang war break out in the valley. You see, St James come like a big amphitheatre – the sea in front, the mountains behind – so every noise does bounce and come back louder. More drums go be starting up soon enough. Nobody eh sleeping tonight. But for me, that normal, because I eh sleep in a month. If Shiva was here, he woulda point he finger and say: *Yes, Mammy, no rest for the wicked!*

But he not here. He dead as Ali-Asgar; onliest difference is my Shiva eh bury yet. And that's what bothering me this whole month: how to send my son to rest in peace? When I-self wasn't at peace with my son. I wasn't on good terms with Shiva, neither he wife; I did stop going by them long time – must be five years now. We was living like strangers.

'Aunty, everybody else in that Karbala desert was big people who coulda fend for theyself. But them soldiers watch a baby and just murder it? When Jameel tell me that story, I cry, you know.'

'You *must* cry,' I say, and in the darkness, under this low-watt green bulb, I take a chance and let my own tears run wild from cheek to jaw, like carailli vine on a rusting fence. 'Lord, was murder, in truth.'

Forgive me for the man Shiva grow to be! A man who stab he wife dead in front their chirren then drink poison and murder he-self, all because she wanted to leave him. Since it happen, I eh leave this house. To come out and go anywhere, I woulda have to walk down the hill, past all my neighbours; I woulda have to walk wondering if they done put two and two together and realise the latest murder-man in the news is *my* son. Wonder if they calling me La Diablesse, a devil-woman who does breed beast or if they still watching me as just a innocent ex-jammette. And even if I get past *my* neighbours, then I woulda have to walk past the cemetery where, rumour have it, all Shiva neighbours done chip in and bury he wife. And even-self I get past the cemetery, then, to turn left is to face Forensics where Shiva still lying down, waiting for me to claim him. To turn right is to face the crematorium where he always say he did want to go ('No worm must eat me, Mammy. Just burn my ass.'). So, forty days I asking myself: *How to come out from inside of here?*

I so shame.

Sometimes, the shame does be so deep in my belly, it does bend me over and have me on the floor, twitching up like fits. Yes, we wasn't on good terms, me and Shiva, but a mother does feel guilty for everything bad in she chirren life; whether they do it or receive it, she does feel is *she* fault.

Sheldon say, 'I wish I could go back in time and fight for the lil boy. You know wha' I mean, Aunty?'

And, instantly, I wonder if is Allah sending message in code: *Pinkie, if you don't fight whatever it is keeping you from your boy-child, if you don't go down there and claim him, who go do it? Time ticking.*

Is true. I used to brush a old police from CID, so I know them fridge-and-them in Forensics barely working. I know Government can't keep Shiva long, maybe one more week; then is plywood box and pauper funeral. Rotten and stinking. No headstone, no name.

I bolt from the chair, lean over the banister and retch . . . but only water coming up. Belly too empty.

'W'happen Aunty?' Sheldon rubbing my back and I coldsweating. 'Must be gas. Look, sip the sweet-drink,' he say.

I wipe my mouth on my duster sleeve and take the cup. Sheldon know I does only drink old-time, glass-bottle Cokes – not the horse piss they selling in plastic bottle – so he does buy six every week and bring for me. More than Shiva ever do. I always used to feel that boy had me in he craw, and he father used to chook thing in he brain against me. And is he father whey force my son to marrid that country-bookie girl who come to Town, get bright and make Shiva run me like dog from their yard.

Still, I sorry. Every woman have a right to go. Why he *kill* the girl?

The Cokes burn slow, going down, till a different question pop in my head. 'But, Shel, how you end up by Jameel, for him to tell you the Hosay story?'

He was delivering fabric, he say, for Jameel-and-them to make their flags and big tadjahs for Hosay. 'Them was now knocking the wood-frames together. I make a joke and say if it have Small Hosay and Big Hosay parade, it should have "Medium Hosay" for half-breed like me to party. But the man get irate, *oui*! Call me ignorant and make me listen the whole history.'

A grunt drop out my mouth. I agree with Jameel: young people ignorant bad. But is who make them to be so . . . ent is old people? That's the question I can't escape: What *I* ever do to make Shiva so ignorant till he want to kill? And I keep coming back to one answer: is not me, is he father have him so. Yes, I coulda bring Shiva to live with me here, but I don't see how that woulda work. A boy should never watch he mother making fares. A boy should never know. That's why I did always keep my two worlds separate. It easier for people to love half-pound, rather than the whole weight of you.

'Then, Jameel invite me to build with them,' Sheldon still explaining. 'If you see how them men does sacrifice – so much nights building tadjah and tuning drum in fire – all for their God. Tonight, I go be pushing a small tadjah that I build. Come and watch me, nah, Aunty? It go help you.'

I study him hard. I start to wonder if he know 'bout Shiva, if somebody tell him that was he own family on the front page of every papers. Me eh think anybody inside here know – nobody say boo to me – except my favourite-sister; she did knock quiet quiet on the door one day and say, 'Pinkie, girl, I sorry.' And she wouldn't run she mouth. She know I never like all the marish and the parish in my private affairs.

I refuse Sheldon invitation. Silence fall. I puff my cigarette; he puff he joint. We exhale the same: aiming the smoke from the house. We know how to stay outta people way. That's what I used to do when I was young: when my sister-them cuss and kick me here, I used to go there by Shiva and he father; and when he father cuss and kick me there, I used to come back here, by my sister-them. Bob and weave; is so I live.

Prrrrrrrat-ta-ta-ta-taat! Somewhere down the hill, another tassa drum roll.

Sheldon say, 'Them-fellas warming up.'

'I hear,' I say, and my mind follow the drum echo. I thinking 'bout what did happen after Shiva last daughter born. Three months straight, that baby *screel* out she lungs. I did keep telling Shiva wife, 'This child born with a caul; she seeing spirit. Let me carry she by a pundit to get jharay.' And one day, I did pick up the child to go, but the wife start bawling for Shiva. He run from the garden, grab the child and say, 'You playing best-grandmother? *You?* The worst mother ever? Go! Nobody want you here!'

Them is the last words my son ever tell me.

How I could barge in Forensics, saying, 'I name Mother. I want my son'? He didn't want me in life; why he go want me in death? I know my place.

'So, you turning Muslim now?' I say, trying to swing the conversation, and my own thoughts, back towards Sheldon and the tadjah he so proud of.

'Nah, Aunty. I-and-I would never betray Jah. But when I listen Jameel, my heart start gnashing. I had-was to do something with the downful vibes. I had-was to either break something or build something, you overstand? So I build that pretty pretty baby tomb, and it make me feel better.'

I nod, again and again, because I know that same feeling: sadness that trying to claw through your chest, restlessness chooking you to do something, but you not sure what or how.

Sheldon slide off the banister and stand up. He biting he lip and watching me sheepish as he say, 'I hadda leave now to help them-fellas. But . . . you go come tonight? It go do you plenty good, Aunty.'

Poor heart, like he sense in he spirit: Aunty Pinkie have plenty plenty things she need to bury. He sense I need a funeral more than anybody else in St James tonight.

'I go come, Shel,' I say, without fully believing it, but I know that deep down I *wants* to come out from here, and I know if I could even-self crawl out tonight, maybe tomorrow I could stand up in broad daylight.

I drag the grip from under my bed – old-style grip: cardboard and vinyl, with metal corners. Pa used to call it he 'valise'. Inside, have all my important business. Me eh open it long time, but tonight, I searching for something – not sure what; I go know when I see it – but I just feeling that the way out this house tonight is not through the front door or back door: is through the past.

The latch spring open. I lift the lid sl-o-o-w like opening a crypt, like I expecting a evil jumbie. But nothing happen. Scatter 'round, it have some mildew-white envelopes with a setta fading studio pictures: Ma in she best frock, Pa in he one suit, me and my sisters in we dan-dan when we was small, even Baba Khan, my grandfather who did come off the last Indian ship; watch him in he dhoti and jacket.

Now, look the envelope with only pictures of me – pictures nobody ever see, except me and the man whey take them. When Pa did carry me in Town for the first time, was to pay rent by we landlord, old Mr. Stone, and I was thirteen years. And when Mr Stone call me in the back, I did went because Pa say, 'Go, beti.' And that day, and every month after that, Mr Stone used to make me lie down on he office couch, and, starting from my head, the man used to sniff me straight down to in-between my toe-them. In all the years, till he dead, Mr Stone never touch me no other way; he never feel me up; he never sex me. He only used to smell me and then pose me and take picture with he big Black camera. That's all. Until I did get to like it – being worship by this old white man, with he red jiggly face and he trembling hand so prune-up as if whole day he jookin' clothes in tub instead of counting cash behind desk. But I couldn't show the man that I like it. He did steady telling me, 'Don't be afraid,' because is frighten self he did want me – 'shy and demure', he used to say – just how he meet me.

But now, I come so old; things change: nowadays, I does frighten to feel exposed.

Inside a long manila folder, I find the deed paper for this property: 33 Terre Brulée Road. From Mr. Edward Stone to me, Pinkie Khan. This coulda be Shiva own. I never tell he wotless father 'bout this, and I never tell *he* neither. I did hold back because I didn't want no man – not even my son – to love me for land. But now, I eh know what go happen when I dead; it go be one setta commess: somebody go find this paper, and then they go hadda find Shiva chirren – the boy and two girls. I sure the wife family take them. Wherever they is, though, I staying far. Ent that's what Shiva wanted? I's over sixty years now; I can't fight up again for chirren love. I go make do with Sheldon alone.

My hand fall on a plastic bag. As I loose the knot, a smell hit me. Baby powder. I pull out a vest with blue piping and press it to my nose. I did put this on Shiva to bring him home after he born. I dip again and find the plastic ID-band the nurse-them had on him. Watch how small it is, nah! Hard to believe a man hand does start off so small and then grow so big it could damage a body. This was the first time my child name ever get use in this world. I read it out now, 'Shiva Gopaul,' and the sound cause that trembling again, deep in the ravine between my chest and my belly as if my butchette drop or I take in with naara strain.

I shub the ID-band in my duster pocket, not sure why, but I feeling like I have to carry it with me tonight to that parade.

And now, a next bracelet on my mind. I shifting things until I glimpse the old 'Y de Lima & Co' box. *Oui-papa*! In one blink, I see all the man I ever truly love parading through my mind Indian file: Shiva, Pa, Mr. Stone and Baba Khan. He was the best jeweller in Coolie Town; de Lima used to send for him whenever they had big-shot clients who want 'exquisite' things. That's how this bera get make. I take it out the box and heft it – so heavy, the gold bright, the rod thick like my little finger and glittering with carailli cut-diamond pattern; then each head is a globe swirling upward to a point, like the dome of a tadjah or even the great Taj Mahal. What a bracelet! I remember the store did order it for a client who never pay, so Baba Khan keep it because is the first one he make with this design, and he didn't know if he would ever make something so perfect again. He did give Pa, and Pa give me. And when I did make Shiva, I hold the same lil plastic ID-band and promise he newborn ears that, when he come a big man, I woulda give him this bera instead. But one day, one day congotay! – that day never come.

I drop the bera in my next duster pocket – it going parade too! And I have no time to ask myself why because a fresh setta hurt start collecting in my chest, like somebody turn on a stand-pipe full blast. I open my mouth to cry out, but my throat have a pressure valve that lock off while my eye-rim overflowing. Then – *Bam, Bam, Bam!* – somebody pound the door.

'Aunty Pinkie! Sheldon say you walking with we to watch Hosay! You ready?'

With the sheet hem, I wipe my face. I hurry to close the grip. Stop crying now; I need my energy to walk out this house and do something with this bera and this ID-band – I not sure what the hell yet – but I know I go feel better afterwards.

Is midnight, and we heading downhill: down Terre Brulée Road, down Bournes Road. Them chirren – my niece-and-nephew-and-them – talking a setta shit 'bout Sheldon.

I hearing them, eh, but I not listening. I feeling so strange since I leave the house. Is like everything around me, things I seeing my whole life, looking so weird like I watching them for the first time. Is like St James grow big big over the forty days I was inside. Every lamppost taller; every streetlight higher. Till the night come like a roof over a mansion for giants, and I's a midget on this pavement. I so lost, me eh even notice when we pass the cemetery.

One of my nephew say, 'Sheldon not stupid. This hadda have profit in it for him.' A next one say, 'Must be some Muslim girl he tracking . . .'

Steups! This modern generation believe in scheme and con. They can't believe somebody could just have a good heart and decide to sacrifice for somebody else. Hear them talking big as if they wise, but they don't even know where the roof over they head come from. Is *me*. It come from me. Pa did always tell me, 'If Stone ever ask what you want, say you want to own where your navel string bury. He ha' plenty land; he could gi' you this one easy.' So I was ready when the opportunity did come, when Mr. Stone take in sick and send for me one last time. I was seventeen when I ask for the land and them pictures; he give me without a fight. I over-cry when that man dead a few months after; I did studying *who go love off on me so again?* Then I did meet Shiva father by the laundry, and, to this day, I feel I woulda never put myself with *he* if I wasn't still grieving Mr. Stone, and I woulda never ever stay if I didn't get pregnant with Shiva. I didn't want the child until he come out, and I watch he, and he watch me, and I feel this is the one man who go be worth any sacrifice, even my own soul.

We reach we usual spot: the traffic light opposite Luckput Street. Small crowd, just like any other Small Hosay. Is only die-hards on these first few nights of Muhurram month. Most people only interested in tomorrow night, Big Hosay, with all the big tadjah that almost touching the telephone wire. You see, most people could only understand *BIG* things. But, simple as you see me here, dumb and stupid with no education, I know it not good to scorn small things. Small things carry plenty goodness, press down like seed. You never know what hiding inside a small thing. I know, though – I been small all my life.

Suddenly, in the nearish distance, I hear tassa: small drums rolling (*prrrraat-ta-ta- ta-taat*) and cymbals chiming (*ching-cha, ching-cha, ching, ching*).

In one pocket, I grab Shiva ID-band; in the next pocket, I slip on the bera. I feeling like I in between baby-Shiva and man-Shiva, holding on to both same time.

'They coming.' Somebody say it; then everybody repeat, 'They coming . . . they coming . . .' and people start craning to see down the road, and the night start to change, and the air start to crackle like fire.

'Who in front?' I ask my niece. 'Jameel Yard supposed to be first. That's the order from since I small.'

'Me eh know, Aunty. I only seeing the tassa boys.'

'Look behind. Check the flag-them on the kathiya platform. What colour flag you seeing most? Purple?'

'Yeah, I think so.'

'That's Jameel Yard. Sheldon with them. He coming.'

My heart pick up a pace. Breeze twirling my dress, I's a lil girl again: standing up beside Baba Khan watching Firepass ritual, hearing the drums and feeling excited and scared same time because I know God about to pass and touch some people, and it have a chance I could be one, and I want that, but I don't want it same time 'cause I don't know what He go want me do in return. 'Pick a drum,' Baba Khan used to tell me, 'and listen it good. It go talk one of these days and tell you what God want.'

'They coming!'

The drummers near enough for me to feel the dhol, the big bass make from tree trunk and goat skin, vibrating through my body. My heart start to pump in time – *dhung-dunk, dhung-dunk* – and my lungs turn harmonium. Ever since I small, I did always like this feeling, this oneness with something powerful. For me, big drum was always the closest thing to God – although, it never really say nothing to me.

But tonight, I pick the small drum. Or rather, I feel when the small drum pick me. It happen just now: the moment them tassa boys change their rhythm from the slowness of the 'Marching Hand' to the fastness of the 'War Hand' that supposed to make everybody think of the Battle in Karbala. The drum say, 'Pinkie! Is war! Is war!'

Well, I shock, *oui*! I born and bred in St James; I see countless Hosay and a good few Firepass, but a drum never talk my private business before. Yes, is *war* self I been fighting this last month, war between the love I still have for my boy-child – the eight-pounds baby I did born from between my two nashy leg – and the disgust I feeling for the man he turn out to be. War, between this feeling that I coulda do something different as a mother and this knowing that you does make chirren, but you don't make their mind. Is war! I start to shake. Everybody shaking because tassa playing, and their body want to dance, but I shaking different. I shaking from a war that want to fling me down in the road, just how it had me fling down on my bedroom floor whole month, and pappyshow me for everybody to see my vulgar shame.

I falling but – *quick!* – I drop everything in my pocket and grab my niece on one side and my nephew on the next.

'You ok, Aunty?'

No time to answer. The tassa boys reach alongside: every man have a cloth round he neck holding he drum, and he forehead frown, and he lip press, and he two drumstick lashing the goatskin like he killing the poor animal again. And every roll getting longer – *prrrraat, prrrrrrraaat* – like the drum begging now, 'Pinkieeee, doh fall down! Time to stand up for your childddd!'

I glimpse the kathiya now, the silky flags fluttering and mirroring streetlight. Then the drum-hand change again; it slow down lil bit, just as the kathiya reach where I could see it in full: a square platform surrounded by flag poles but, in the middle, a small tadjah resembling a wedding cake, when is really a tomb. The white walls, the domes shaped like the ends of the bera in my pocket, the crescent moon and shimmering star. Yes, is just cardboard and paint, glue and paper, but it looking like it build from magic and love.

'Sheldon!' somebody call.

And is true, he right there, behind the kathiya, wheeling it forward. He have on the same black track pants and t-shirt from when I did see him earlier. He right: is a funeral. All of we shoulda be wearing on black.

'Dougla-Gong!' somebody say, and Sheldon wave. Then he spot me and – *voosh!* – he dash over.

'Aunty Pinkie, you really come!' He hug me tight and lift me off the ground. And that's when the drum talk again: *Let go the child, so you could bury the man.*

I whisper in Sheldon ears-hole. 'Go with the tadjah by the sea later.'

He put me down and say, 'Ok,' but he eye-them groping my face like they trying to find the door in a wall.

'Take this,' I say, and I fold Shiva ID-band into Sheldon palm. 'Chook it inside the tomb before allyuh push it out to sea.'

'Ok,' he say again, but this time he eye steady, so I know he understand. 'I go do that for you, Aunty. I promise.'

He run back to the kathiya. It passing us now, but he glancing back at me and smiling. The tassa hand change again, get even slower. I recognise this rhythm and remember the name from Muslim school: The Hands of Sorrow.

They does beat this rhythm to symbolise the Battle done.

Well, I lean on the traffic light, and right here on the Western Main Road, I spread open my heart and surrender. The sadness ease out wet and gentle, like when you peeing down yourself in a dream. And the dream I seeing is the future – what Sheldon go do by the sea later. I don't need to be there to see it; I could stay right here because I done see it happen so much times in the past. He and some next fella go jump out the pickup truck but leave on the low beam to shine a path to the water. Sheldon go hold one side of the base, and the next fella go hold the 'nother side, and they go lift the tadjah out the tray and walk, in the light, down to the shore. Then he go say, 'Wait, bai,' and they go rest it down so he could pull off he sneakers and hoist he track pants as high as it could go. Then, they go walk into the sea with the tadjah. They go walk careful, careful, feeling with they foot. They go walk as far as the beam from the van could stretch, and when water hit them high enough, they go float the tadjah and push it 'way into the Gulf. And it go make the water ripple for a minute, and, in the van light, it go look like is God zipping open the black sea. But wet cardboard and paper don't take long to sink. Blink twice, it go disappear: a watersoak tomb for two innocent lil baby: Ali-Asgar, the Prophet great-grandson, and Shiva Gopaul, Pinkie Khan onliest son.

'Look the next Yard coming!' somebody say, and is so I remember where I is. Yes, it still have six more tombs to parade, but I done get through with the first one.

Now is time to bury the man. Not everything could clean off in water; some things does take fire. So Baba Khan did say, a time when we was watching Firepass, and I did ask him why so much people does walk them red-hot coals. Shiva did always insist he want to cremate. Maybe he did know a secret that the rest of we didn't know. Maybe he did understand that he had something inside him that needed to burn 'way for he soul to come pure gold.

I will go for him tomorrow. But I have two stops to make first: one by the crematorium to find out the price and one to pawn the bera to pay that price.

And this time I don't want it back. This time, it go belong to my son.

7

Having a Black point of view

- How do we choose which point of view to use for our writing?

- You control what the reader will feel and experience.

- Think about who is telling the story.

- Consider what they can see and know.

There are various points of view we can use in our writing, and we are going to explore which one would suit the story we are telling. Apart from looking at first, second, omniscient and third-person limited, we can quickly consider viewpoint before we move on to point of view. This is especially important for Black writers and characters so that we can make sure we are not falling into the trap of using a view from a dominant culture. As writers, we explore who the point of view belongs to before it is given to the character and the writing. Depending on our own histories, we could need to interrogate where we receive our information about ourselves and the world around us. So, before we settle on a point of view for our story, we need to understand the viewpoint of our character's information.

If we study or studied English literature throughout school, we would have read books with a worldview that may not be our own. We must be conscious of who is telling the story and what that character knows and understands of their world. This doesn't mean we can't have characters who carry a viewpoint that doesn't fit with their circumstances. I once worked with a student who was writing their law degree thesis about immigrants and the problems they were causing in the UK. This student was a second-generation immigrant. Her family had migrated and worked hard to let her attend university and study law. This student had gained her viewpoint from reading newspapers and listening to particular opinions on the television or radio. It took some gentle questioning and guided readings for her to understand that her viewpoint was perhaps skewed by what she was hearing. Likewise, our characters will be products of their environment, and it is for us as writers to decide which narrative we want our story to give. We need to consider viewpoint when building our character profile.

Now let's explore the different points of view we can deploy in our writing.

First person

This can feel very immediate. We're walking through the story with the character. Everything we know and learn is from the character's experience. We can only know what they know. Although sometimes we can read between the lines. It's also helpful when there is dialogue or another character impacts the story significantly. But even then we will only have our first-person point of view to get a feel of what is happening. I like first person. Once we know who the character is and they're telling us a good story, we can get involved with them. We can understand how they feel and what their worldview is. We might not agree with everything they tell us, but we can understand it. Until we start to feel that maybe they aren't really being truthful and faithful to what is happening. At that point we must ask if we can trust the character and their account of the story. We can question whether they are they are telling us truths. Are they an unreliable narrator? What has swayed their way of thinking? Have their life experiences made them look at the world in a particular way?

We must remember that 'I' is not the author. 'I' is the character that has been created. We have developed our character and their voice, and we know the language they use. We put them on the page, and they tell their story as they know it.

'I' lets the reader experience the world through the character and hear their thoughts. When we are using the first-person point of view, we must know our character and understand their worldview.

Example 1

Good morning! Let me introduce myself. My name is Dora Chance. Welcome to the wrong side of the tracks.

Put it another way. If you're from the States, think of Manhattan. Then think of Brooklyn. See what I mean? Or, for a Parisian, it might be a question of rive guache, rive droite. With London, it's the North and South divide. Me and Nora, that's my sister, we've always lived on the left-hand side, the side the tourist rarely sees, the bastard side of Old Father Thames . . .

. . . What would have become of us, if Grandma hadn't left us this house? 49 Bard Road, Brixton, London, South West Two. Bless this house. If it wasn't for this house, Nora and I would be on the streets by now, hauling our worldlies up and down in plastic bags, sucking on the bottle for comfort like babes unweaned, bursting into songs of joy when finally admitted to the night shelter and therefore chucked out again immediately for disturbing the peace, to gasp and freeze and finally snuff it disregarded on the street and blow away like rags. That's a thought for a girl's seventy-fifth birthday, what?

ANGELA CARTER, *Wise Children* (1992), 1

This example gives us a very strong voice and character. We know that we are going to be entertained because of the irreverent narration. However, we may come to a point where we question whether or not we can trust this narrator, whether she is reliable or unreliable. But that isn't a bad thing!

Example 2

A grey mouse was wriggling in a wire noose on the hallway floor. I stepped over it, tapped the frosted glass of the office doors and entered. Albert glanced up at me from between two piles of papers. He picked up his fountain pen and began signing off letters, signing and blotting, signing and blotting, all the while sucking on a pear drop that hung pink on his tongue like an extra nipple. Behind him. The windowpanes shook. Twin jack hammers were breaking rubble on the bombed-out plot adjacent to us. It was a frantic, anxious time in London, good for insurance companies. Albert's shirt was blotchy with sweat, an effect of the building's addled central heating.

I was waiting expectantly. He shuffled his mouth nipple to one side.

PETER KALU, 'The Fall of the House of
Penhryn', in Glimpse (2022), 179

We are given an insight into the character and their concerns. The things that they notice gives information about the setting, the other character, the era the story takes place.

Example 3

Me like that girl ever since me meet her on me doorstep in the rain and bring her inna me house. Me decide me really like she fi Tyrone.

She talk to me nice an respeckful; seh her madder from Wales and her fadder from one of them small island, though she never tell me which one. Perhaps me never ask.

She waiting outside of me door two hours fi Tyrone. Inna the cold! You nuh call that love?

Me tell her, seh, never mind sweetheart, me warm you up with a nice cuppa cocoa.

Nice girl yuh see? Pretty nuh rarse. She got long eyelash – no false ting dat – and she eye dem big and lovely like cat eye. The way she look at me: nice smile, nice teet – I see she lickle shy.

Me really like that girl fi me son.

JACOB ROSS, 'Raising Tyrone', in
Tell No-one About This (2017), 281

This example is in first person but also shows how the language works to add texture. The author has stayed consistent with the way he has spelled words. We get a distinct view of the narrator through the things she is narrating, and we also see things about her character that are unsaid.

Second person

There are several ways that second person is used in stories. Using second person often makes the reader complicit with the action. The narrator is talking directly to the reader, telling them what they are doing or have done. Second person can also be used for the character/narrator to talk to another character 'off-stage': imagine a dead ancestor or an ex-lover. It can also be used for the character/narrator to address themselves in the third person. It is absolutely more than just using the pronoun 'you' and requires us to be performative in our writing. It takes a lot of skill and reading other literature written in this point of view to pull it off well. The reader is pulled into the world when it is done skilfully.

Example 1

Something is wrong with you. They keep telling you that because you burn to break through the iron door and go flying across the gravel-yard, over the wire fence into the sun.

What will they say if you tell them that this month the rainbirds sing their last songs and the yam-shoots will come snaking from the earth, redder than blood from a fresh-cut finger?

. . . The river will be bright with sunshine. The stone on which you like to sit and watch the girls come on Fridays to laugh and tease and do their washing is cool.

The girls make fun of you – the boys too, who gather like Blackbirds on the bank to stare at Ela, Jenny, Sara, Pansy, standing wet and almost bare in the pools, pounding clothes on the stones.

JACOB ROSS, 'The Understanding', in
Tell No-one About This (2017), 39

The narration is almost the character telling themselves what others have said about them. It adds a layer of safety and of interest to the telling. Is there a split in personality?

Example 2

Growing up is hard. You know this. And when your mother has X-ray eyes and dances like a wobbling bag of water? When your father's idea of fun is to put all your money in a savings account and make you get up at 5 am every Sunday morning? When Kenny, Percival Thorton High's big show-off, is after Christina Parker – your Christina Parker? And when you have a shrimp of a little sister who is the bawlingest little six year old girl in the whole of Riverland? Then growing up is something you're not sure you can manage at all. Who in their right mind could? Who? You?

A-DZIKO SIMBA GEGELE, *All Over Again* (2022), 1

This example distinctly gives us the feeling that the narrator is addressing themselves in the third person. Perhaps trying to make sense of their situation by giving it to the reader, then at the end asking the reader to consider the situation.

Example 3

You wear a bracelet. Your bracelet is an amulet. Your bracelet is a talisman. It is a beautiful silver heavy bracelet that is as old as the continent of Africa. Black pharaohs have worn your bracelet.

The men enter your classroom in the name of art, bringing their smells of poverty, their smells of insecurity.

. . . Why have you worn such an alluring piece of jewellery in a place like this?

RONNIE MCGRATH, 'Contraband', in *Glimpse* (2022), 60

In this example the narrator is talking to a character 'off-stage' and as the story continues the narrator uses 'I' and therefore becomes a character in the story. An interesting technique that enhances the story and brings another layer to the second-person point of view.

Third-person omniscient

There are two ways we can approach the third-person point of view. One is through the omniscient narrator who can report anything and everything to the reader. This narrator is god-like. They take the place of the writer and can tell us anything that interests them. We get informative asides, we know what a character is thinking and doing in another room or another city. The omniscient narrator knows all. This is more an original way of storytelling. Before stories were written down there would be a storyteller who told stories. This switched to the author and the omniscient narrator. Think of it almost like watching a movie where the camera moves between characters and gives us an overview of the story.

Example 1 – omniscient

Elsie was with Gaspard, her live-in renal-failure patient, when her ex-husband called to inform her that his girlfriend, Olivia, had been kidnapped in Port-au-Prince. Elsie had just fed Gaspard some cabbage soup when her cell phone rang. Gaspard was lying in bed, his head carefully propped on two pillows, his bloated and pitted face angled toward the bedroom skylight, which allowed him a slanted view of a giant coconut palm that for years had been leaning over the lakeside house in Gaspard's single-family development.

Elsie pressed the phone between her left ear and shoulder and used her right hand to wipe a lingering piece of cabbage from Gaspard's chin. Waving both hands as though conducting an orchestra, Gaspard signaled to her not to leave the room while motioning for her to carry on with her conversation.

EDWIDGE DANTICAT, 'Dosas', in
Everything Inside (2020), 3

This example is clearly watching the scene from above. We can see how the narrator tells us what both characters are doing and also what their actions mean.

Example 2 – omniscient

Four months after Jesse left for Kingston to find a husband, Ma Lou' grandson Devonshire came home from Colón. Strutted in was more like it. He arrived in full-blown Colón style – a brown draped suit, complete with watch chain with dangling charms and a fat gold watch inside his fob pocket, matching brown derby, yellow boots, and a walking-stick with the head of a wolf carved in ivory on the handle. 'Dev what a sweet-man you turn into,' Mama laughed when trailing the sweet smell of brilliantine he came into the bedroom to pay his respect to her the minute he arrived. It was the first time in years Brid had heard her mother laugh.

OLIVE SENIOR, 'Window', in *Discerner of Hearts* (1995), 57

This narrator is seeing all and reporting it from their point of view. Look at the length of the sentences and notice that this is a distinct voice for the narrator. They are telling us information that they deem important for the story.

Third-person limited

I must admit, this may be my personal favourite point of view to use in storytelling. This is because it gives me the benefit of close contact with the character, whilst maintaining a respectable distance. That's not to say I don't use other points of view; I use what the story demands. In limited, we can be with the character who is telling the story. We can state their thoughts and their actions, similar to first person but with an added bonus. Whereas in first person it would seem strange for the character to tell us what they are doing and why, for example, 'I sat down in my favourite chair and rubbed my hand across the leather.' That feels a little over the top because we don't narrate ourselves like that. With third-person limited I could use, 'she sat down carefully. It was her favourite chair and she sighed as she ran her hand across the leather, appreciating its coolness.'

So, as you can see, third-person limited is still following the character's actions and dipping into their mindset but can naturally add some extra details. I use this point of view when I want to be with the character intimately, but I want a natural way of giving extra details.

Example 1 – limited

The traffic was really heavy. She hated coming to Reddish. It was a nightmare on match days now that Man City had moved from Maine Road. And of course today was a match day. The place had become scruffy. There were closed down shops along the main road. The furniture stores still had the same old shit outside, covered in layers of dust. She couldn't understand why her mum wouldn't move over to somewhere in South Manchester. It wasn't like she couldn't afford it. Her house was massive, the mortgage paid off ten years before. She could easily get a small flat out in West Didsbury or somewhere like that.

The feeling of dread was working its way through her system. It started in her bladder area – her root chakra according to Anna – then clomped through her innards in wooden clogs until it reached her solar plexus. It was a little bit like when her cat padded on her lap, only this was inside and the cat was a lion wearing steel toecaps.

'What ya grinning at, Sis?'

'I was thinking about cats. In workmen's boots.'

MULI AMAYE, 'Streamlining', in *Closure* (2015), 144

In this story we can see how I've used the third-person limited. Had I chosen first-person point of view, there would have been some details missing because the character wouldn't tell us what they were thinking in so much detail.

Example 2 – limited

He made it through the scripture reading and opening prayer. He even maintained his smile when the Deacon reminded everyone of the night's theme: 'Saving Marriages, One Soul at a time.' That's when Declan glanced around and noticed the male–female–male–female seating configuration: the audience was composed of couples.

He grunted and locked his arms across his chest, debating if to feel tricked or not. Ruth had made it sound like an ordinary Night Service, like they were just coming to pray; she hadn't mentioned the sermon would be focused on marriage. But then again, Declan considered, this was appropriate for a couple celebrating their fifth anniversary. And by now, Ruth surely knew better than to think she could convert him. What she didn't know, Declan smirked inwardly, was that he was intent on her re-conversion – back to Michelle – tonight.

CELESTE MOHAMMED,
Pleasantview (2021), 148

This example also shows how third-person limited, whilst following the character, Declan, enables the reader to be aware of more than if Declan was narrating in the first-person point of view. For example, he wouldn't narrate 'I smirked inside' because that would just be weird!

Discussion point

- How do we decide what point of view to use for our stories?

- Do we need to create a character who is the narrator for third-person point of view?

- When would second-person point of view work best?

Exercise

I suggest you take your time with this exercise; you will be tempted to just rush it off by changing pronouns, but we need more than that.

Write an opening couple of paragraphs for a short story. Think about character and voice and language. Don't forget how we use sentence length and the senses. Decide where the setting is, even if we don't get to see it at the opening.

- Write the first version in first person. Use the 'I'. Let your character take us into the beginning of the story.

- Rewrite it in second person. Decide who the 'you' is going to be addressed to; this will help you decide what needs to be narrated. You can use the same character as the first-person point of view and if you know that character you will know whether they are talking to the reader, an off-stage character or themselves.

- Rewrite it again in third-person omniscient. This will give us a broad overview of what is happening and more details of the setting. We can even travel around a bit and find out what is happening elsewhere.

- Rewrite it again in third-person limited. Let the narrator step inside the character and tell us things that the character wouldn't think to tell in first person.

Really consider what it is you must change to make it work. Ask yourself which point of view works best for the story you're telling. Take notice of which one feels more comfortable for you to write in. Enjoy it!

Round up

There are different points of view for our writing that each tell the story in a different way.

We still consider our character's viewpoint and where that came from because that's all part of our character development.

Point of view is the way in which we tell our stories and what we want our readers to access, depending on the story we are telling.

We can take our time and try different points of view, especially if we find that a story isn't working in the way we want it to. Changing from first person to third-person limited will open the story in a new way. Changing from third person to first person will take us closer to the character so that we only see and know what they see and know. Experimenting with different points of view will help our writing to grow.

Read

The following short story, 'Boss Lady', is a great example of point of view from a third-person limited point of view. Read it and consider what we would know if it was first person and what would be missing. Think about how the third-person limited allowed us to have the voice, the language and the characterization of Misha. Consider what point of view you would have written this story from and decide why you would have chosen that. What would it add to the story?

'Boss Lady'

Nadja Nabbie

Dress. Misha have no idea about dress. Even as he search through the sale racks. Checking them over and over again like when he does pick the lice crawling through he bowl cut hair. He stubby fingers insisting. It forcing him to hunt. Further and further, Misha finding he self in worlds of satin, chiffon and lace needing to find it. Is determine the man determine.

'De puhfect dress fuh de puhfect gyal.'

Is what he want to write on the card. He done make up he mind. It have no two ways about it.

He done stay up all night planning the 'big moment'. He done decide where and when it go happen. All the nice thing he go whisper in she ear. The big hand gestures he going and make before dropping to he knee and pulling out the ring to propose to he woman, he boss lady, Maribel de Freitas.

He eh leaving the mall till he find it, inno. The usual walk-through Port-ah-Spain not going to do at all. At all. This is not some plain Jane or some Miss Ordinary. She is not a gold digger or some sketel skinning she ass all over social media for everybody to see. This is Maribel. She have to have the best.

Sweat from he sticky palms pour out onto empire waistlines and A-lines, sweetheart cuts and V-necks, straps and tubes.

'It go fix everything,' he mutter to he self over and over as he speed from one store to the next like a animal escaping capture.

It have to fix the thing. In fact, it have no other choice cause it have no ending thing with she.

Not at all.

He does strangle them thought every time they appear. Sometimes first, pinning them with nail and then slicing their stomach wide open like he used to do with the garden lizards and frog when he was a child.

It have no ending thing with she. Not at all.

The proposal have to be large and in charge. Something big enough to win she over and warm up she heart so she could smile big and he go feel nice.

After they last argument, about two months ago, she gone quiet quiet on him. She does push him off when he nudge she for morning kiss and she doh respond when he pet she light light in the night. In fact, Misha does have to pretend the shadowy outline of she skin real and is then he does walk he hands on the wall to touch it, scraping he knuckles against the grainy concrete and peeling paint.

He go fix it. He go fix it and it go all be ok.

'Thing go go back to normal. To how they used to be. The fire go come back and she go realize is I is the real man for she. Not PC Williams, na. Me. Misha Rajah. Me.'

He walking from shop to shop telling he self that over and over like if he singing ah ole time calypso. When he get to All that Jazz, he straighten he shirt cause it get wet wet with all he nervous sweating. He determined to find that dress inno. And when he find it, he go know. It going and click just like when she come into he life that evening.

* * *

Mist snake through the valley. Misha did find he self tumbling through the thick, thick grass up the top of Chancellor. He was trying all how to escape the city. Smoke spin spider web off the end of he cigarette. He drifting about the bending forest disorderly and as if he drunk.

Is the yellow dress that catch he attention. It they' sprawling on the ground, wide wide like a big ballon. The ends have these bright bright shocks of red.

The girl who was wearing it, she hands decorate with dirt and green grass blades. She ears press into the sounds of the earth.

Is when he see she so, he decide to duck in the bushes so no one go know he there. He ready he self to spy on them. He know she man go come soon, that they going and fuck where they think no one could see them and when all that happening, he go hide here in this place with he own crotch screaming and swelling.

Hours did pass but she remain alone. The man ain't never show up, na.

Is only when Misha did realize something wrong, is then he say he going and check the scores further. He wobble and walk toward she body slumping in a strange daze. She doh wear the usual smile he see all the time when he creep on the roof and watch she through the bathroom window at night. The same smile he does dream about all day at work. The one he does think about when he fondling inside he pants in the dead of night.

Instead, she lie down with she tongue on she lip. He lean over to check she and all of a sudden is like the air dry, dry. It disturb in a kind of way. She eh even skin up she nose at the scent of he cheap cologne. He want to say he sorry. He want to say he could make thing better but like the words not coming cause is now he realize what happen and like he can't hide the happiness. The man finally get he chance. He promise to take care of she. Make she a honest woman.

He say, 'Sweetheart, doh study it inno. I go protect you and nobody have to know. That is between me and you, yuh hear? That is big people business.'

Misha know he eh have nothing really to offer. A galvanize roof with holes under that he put some plastic bucket from the Chinese shop to catch the rainwater. He have a few plate and some plastic cup. It have a bed that does creak.

'Listen, is home and at least, yuh go be safe.'

That night they did lie down on the dusty floor with fire erupting on Misha's tongue lapping up on the girl skin.

＊＊＊

Dresses.

Misha smiling bouncing from rack to rack looking for the perfect one. He buzz away all the sales girl them who trying to help him out. He doh need them help. This is for he girl and he alone know what she like. He doh need no help to make this choice.

He inspect all it have in the store. Gown with glitter. Short sequin style. Tight animal print. Every time he hold one, he hold the fabric tight, especially on the waistline excited for the way it go grasp Maribel fleshy hip. He could hear she all now squealing in delight.

'She go know. She go know I is the man for she. Not that stupid police officer.'

He willing to pay the highest price. It doh matter if it cost him half a year of hardware work, just that he want to see she spinning in it like the little dolly that used to pop up in Ma jewelry box, the one he love to look at when he was a child. The one Pa pelt behind Misha little sister head the night she wanted to play big woman and open she mouth for he. He good yank her hair tight and ram himself inside her mouth, and still she scream at him uncontrollably.

* * *

Sweat swell and stick on Misha skin as he lie down inside a weed scented cloud pulling at he lips, spying at he beauty, he boss woman who skin out on the couch head back and in a constant daze.

The only thing though is she lost in another world dreaming of Mr. Officer. Dreaming of the way she does wrap she leg around the man when Misha gone. How she does scream in ecstasy as she sprawl out to receive he strength and confidence. How inside they lust, on the heat of him dripping, she does spread out and lay she head down on he chest and listen to he heart pulsing sweet talk as he roam the length of she leg and whisper all kind of nice thing in she ear.

The dusty fan only whirring heat about the darkness of the room. Misha swat the stench from he cess smelling arm. He desperate to clobber the images of the affair picking at him like if he is a corpse and them thoughts is like vulture only clawing at he sanity.

He have to do something to end this relationship the two of them have going. He have to do something to win she back. Is he fault for being so stupid to think a woman like that could ever like he.

But is what he go do? Is how he go prove he self?

He pull at the top hairs on he head to search for an answer in he mind. Is like he walking around a burial ground looking for an unmarked grave.

An idea pop in he head but he don't like it. Something to do with flowers and chocolate. Real movie style thing. He hear women does like that but he find it too little. He need something more exciting. More grand.

A dinner? A walk in the park? A teddy bear? None of that good enough.

He spot something yellow with blots of red, like hibiscus flowers, peeping at him from the bottom drawer. Is the dress she was wearing that evening he find she face down in the bush. Is then the idea come to him. A proposal. Yes, yes. He need to make she see that he is the one willing to commit to loving she for all of eternity. He sure is that kind of thing that go give him the edge over Mr. 'Play He is Big Time Police'.

He see heself as a hero riding home on a stallion and sweeping she off she feet. Brushing he fists against Mr. Officer face when she realize that man was the villain all this time. Misha go beat he into the ground. Maribel go spit on him when she realize that man was too damn weak.

Misha stand in the darkness of the room with all the fantasies exploding about him and he feel so grand. Today. Today it go happen. He seeing it all come together and with the dress, the ring and the card, everything going to be top tier. Is then he decide: fuck it, he going and make it happen for real. He call in sick at work and head out to the gallery.

A flash of blue light and a siren lurk about the bottom of the street.

Misha know is Mr. Officer. He in the area. He only waiting on Misha to go to work and then he go be up her inside of Maribel but not today. Today Misha going and catch them in the act and when he embarrass the man, Maribel go know Misha is the one for she. He going an win. No matter the cost.

***

Time decomposing.

Minutes crawl from the clock like a roaches over decay. Misha only wiping the flurry of water from he face. He need the dress now or else he go miss he chance. He go lose she completely.

He have to move fast. He racing, pushing aside metal shining hangers to get to the one but everything feeling like it not matching up to she beauty. Nothing good enough to get him the win. He take off he watch and stuff it deep inside he pocket. He can't stand how it only cackling at him.

Misha only wobbling about the store. He hand trembling and mouth quivering. He need it now or else. Gripping he chest and wiping he face, he stop a bit to get steady. He have to get a hold of this fear that unbalancing him. The Officer can't win. Not today. He take a deep breath and gone back to searching, pulling and pulling at different thing but it have nothing. Oh, God, it have nothing. He shove he head in he hand. He can't accept this defeat so, nah. He stop. Take another breath. Start again. He look and he look and is then it happen. He hear the heels knocking on the tiles.

Metal clanking on a rack behind him. He spin around and he see it. A maroon gown with golden bows and heavy, heavy sequin weighing it down and he know – that is it.

He launch forward and grab the thing. Yank it off the hook and head straight to the counter. He watch the time. Fifteen minutes is all he have to make this work. The Officer go be gone any minute now.

Misha race out the busy road and flag down a taxi. He ready now. He tell he self is now the thing start. The taxi man moving good on the road until it have some sirens hollering behind them. Car begin to pull to the side. A road block. Ambulance and three police vehicle. This stinking dutty Trinidad.

Misha can't believe it.

'Huh, is like the man did know my plan?'

Misha know he not too far from home now. He could make it if he put some pace in he steps. He pay the taxi man and pop out and start to run like he in a marathon.

He speed down the bushy back track and then a narrow alley before crossing the festering box drain. The place quiet quiet. He breathe a sigh of relief. Yes, it still have a chance to confront Mr. Officer.

Like a true cartoon prince, Misha run up to the apartment where he and Maribel staying at the top of the hill. He move quick opening the locks and duck in the damp garage before he scamper round the side of the house where it have the broken louvres and rubbish in the yard. He get round the back door and run inside fast.

'Get way from she! That is my woman,' he scream but no one answer. Just that it quiet. Too quiet.

He pacing the apartment searching for Mr. Officer. 'I know yuh hear, inno.' Still, nothing come only the silence. He stop. He confused. He so so damn confused.

He walk in the living room where Maribel on the couch. She head back in the same daze she was in when he left her. She mouth open wide. Flies buzzing round she. Maggot crawling from she green fingers.

'Where he is, eh? Where he is, Maribel? Yuh damn hoe.'

He shouting but she not answering. She just lying down there in the same daze with she mouth wide wide open.

'Oh God. Oh God, what I really say? What I really saying? Baby, I so so sorry eh. I sorry to doubt you. Sorry to think yuh was with another man.'

He anger melting. Heart pouring out with guilt.

Making he way on she lap, he become a puddle of tears begging forgiveness for forgetting the sweetness she is. He let she know is only cause he love she so much he does act so damn chupid sometimes. He start to open the bag with the things he did get from the mall for she. Footsteps come in the room.

'Misha . . . Misha Rajah . . . step away from that body.'

He turn to see Mr. Officer coming from behind the lattice partition with a gun and cuffs.

'Don't move. Raise yuh hands in the air.'

Tears streaming down Misha face like if is river come down. He lose the fight. He can't believe it.

Betray. He get betray. Is nuh me who do it, it was a next man. The boss man at he work who everybody know does interfere with people girl chirren.

He want to say inno but he doh have the words to tell the truth. Instead he let it happen. Let the fate tighten around he wrists as the bag did fall from he hand and the dress slip and slide along with the ring and the card and the words that write neat neat in cursive, *De pufhect dress fuh de puhfect gyal . . . Baby, yuh go marrid meh?*

8

Black story, plot and structure

- Identifying the main elements required to create a story.

- How to create tension, whether through action or emotion, and how the decisions made impact on the storytelling.

- Thinking of traditions of storytelling in African history, we will consider if there is another way in which plot, story and structure can be told.

There are many ways to approach storytelling, but sometimes we get hung up on what is story and what is plot and what are the differences. We can think about it in this way:

- Story = Who, what, where?

- Plot = How, when, why?

This is a simple way of identifying whether our story has a plot or if it's a series of events that don't really go anywhere. I was guilty of this in my first novel. The voice was great, everybody loved the character, 'things' kept happening to the character in different settings, but it didn't hang together as a story and it didn't have a strong plot line.

As a rule, a short story must have structure. It must have the bare bones on which to hang the clothes of the story. It must have a plot, that we have mapped out, so we know how the story happens, when it is happening and why it is happening. More often than not there must be some tension in the storyline, whether this is through action or emotion. So, we don't always need adventure, shootouts, fast car rides and escapades; it works just as well when it is quiet, character-focused and internal.

Quick-fire example

Adel must reach town before the bank closes because she doesn't have enough money for her rent again. Her bank card was chewed by the dog and won't work in the ATM. Her landlord is coming and he threatened to evict her if she's late again. Her car won't start, so she calls an uber. Half-way there it breaks down, so the driver calls for another one. None are close by so he points her in the direction of a busy street where she can flag a taxi. There's 30 minutes to go before the bank closes. She flags down a taxi and someone else jumps in it; she flags another one and it stops. As she's about to get in someone runs up and grabs her bag from her hand and runs off. She becomes hysterical and the car drives off. It's 10 minutes to bank closing time. She has the bank card in her hand and her phone in her pocket. A car pulls up. It's her original uber. He drives her to the bank, and she makes it with 30 seconds to spare. The guard won't let her in. Her landlord is inside and he sees her banging on the door. He says she's with him so the guard lets her in. She gets inside, gets her money and pays her rent.

This is all action and far too much tension. I feel I need to sit this young lady down and give her some advice on organization! But beside that, this is a basic plot squashed into one paragraph. The character is somewhere and wants something, various things stop the character from reaching their goal, the character prevails, is stopped, gives up, something happens, picks up again, resolution. So, the outline is the drawing of this plot (think a camel hump); the story is what the plot is about.

We have an opening, rising action, obstacles, climax or pinnacle of problems, falling action and resolution. These are the main points, but there are plenty of variations of story and plot where these points are not in the same order. For example, the tension can also start at the beginning, so something has happened and we don't yet know what.

We meet the character and the story at the climax or pinnacle or we start with the rising action. Alternatively, we can come in at the resolution stage and this works particularly well when it's something amazing or awful and we wait for the story to unravel to see how the character reached that point. We can also begin at the consequences stage, the falling action, again going backwards until we know how we reached the point the story began for the character.

The conflict in our stories can be mental, emotional or physical, but it needs to be there – something that stops the character from sailing through the story on a fluffy white cloud with angels, rainbows and unicorns. We have to create tension to keep the story engaging and something that moves our character from A to B, whether this is physically or emotionally. Obviously, there are exceptions to the rule and we may have read many quiet stories that seem to lack tension or story or plot, and yet we have been pulled along and read the story to the end. One story for me that caused quite a strong disagreement with my PhD cohort was *Never Let Me Go* by Kazuo Ishiguro. I term this as a quiet book: the writing is beautiful and it flows and there seems to be little tension involved. But for me it was there, for others it was missing everything that makes a story. Subjective, but also made into a movie which somehow vindicates my enjoyment of it!

Exercise 1

Write your own mini story. Your character wants something; several things stop them from getting it; they almost succeed only to be pulled back again; finally there is a resolution. It doesn't have to be perfect; we're just playing around with using conflict to stop our character reaching their goal.

We can now have a look at a couple of examples and attempt to identify the plot and the story within each.

Example 1

The ground had gone from solid paving to the sort of sludge that grew hands and pulled you down by your feet. Cutty tried to steady himself as he stumbled across the damp terrain. Rain and sweat trickled into his eyes, blurring the slick night, while above his head the furious whirr of helicopter blades continued to cut through the black skies. Losing his footing he fell to the ground, and the bullet wound gouged into his thigh screamed in protest. Cutty clenched his teeth and touched the bleeding hole blown into his flesh. Lifting an angry fist he struck the bag strapped to his back and released a burst of coppery scent into the air.

'Don't start with me, boy! I told you to stick to the road. I told you not to go traipsing about where you've got no business traipsing.'

'I wouldn't be out here in the first place if you had stuck to the plan. But you got greedy, wanted all the money for yourself,' Cutty snapped back.

GEORGINA SIMMONS, 'My Brother's Keeper',

in *Shots in the Dark* (2018), 40

This is quite an action-based example. We have joined the story after something has happened. The who, what, where of the story is beginning to develop and the how, when, why of the plot is slowly being revealed.

Example 2

Wash the white clothes on Monday and put them on the stone heap; wash the color clothes on Tuesday and put them on the clothesline to dry; don't walk bare-head in the hot sun; cook pumpkin fritters in very hot sweet oil; soak your little cloths right after you take them off; when buying cotton to make yourself a nice blouse, be sure that it doesn't have gum in it, because that way it won't hold up well after a wash; soak salt fish overnight before you cook it; is it true that you sing benna in Sunday school?; always eat your food in such a way that it won't turn someone else's stomach; on Sundays try to walk like a lady and not like the slut you are so bent on becoming; don't sing benna in Sunday school; you mustn't speak to wharf-rat boys, not even to give directions; don't eat fruits on the street – flies will follow you; but I don't sing benna on Sundays at all and never in Sunday school;

JAMAICA KINCAID, *Girl* (1978)

Still thinking about quiet tension, I like to refer to *Girl* by Jamaica Kincaid: it's a short story and worth reading for an example of emotional tension. You can find a video of Jamaica Kincaid reading the story out loud and also the full story online. On first reading there seems to be little happening. We can ask ourselves where the tension is in this story. But on a careful reading, we feel the heaviness of expectation for this girl child and the confusion that she feels at not being able to make the grade and there being nothing she can do about it. There is a story, who/what/where and a plot how/when/why. And the tension is the emotional toll that becoming a woman will take on this girl.

Conflicting emotions can also cause tension in our stories. When our story is about someone with conflicting emotions – that's the tension – we need to draw that out and explore with our character how to navigate the conflict. For this to happen we need to know our character – think back to character profiles and what shaped our character to become who they are. We then need to give them conflicting desires.

Mini example

Miss Luty is the Sunday school teacher for the local church. She has a favourite student, Jemma, who learns all the Bible verses and helps with the younger children. Miss Luty treats her like a daughter. One day Jemma confides that she thinks she's gay. Miss Luty feels it's her duty to protect the younger children but also, she knows that Jemma is good with them. She feels it's against the teaching of her faith, but she loves Jemma like a daughter and doesn't want to reject her.

This simple dilemma creates tension for our character, Miss Luty, and our plot and storyline could be spent unravelling her thought processes and the conclusion she comes to and why. Alternatively, we could look at this from Jemma's point of view and see where the tension lies for her and what her story is.

Exercise 2

Write a mini story that has emotional conflict for your character. Having a moral dilemma always works, and understanding who your character is will help you to choose the dilemma. Give your character choices, as this will create tension and that in turn will drive the story. Have some fun, you're practising!

Discussion point

- How important is plot?

- What ways can we add tension to our stories?

- Does something big always have to happen to a character?

Structure

Once we have written the first draft of our story and we come to editing, we are going to look for our plot, the outline that the story clothes are hanging on. We have to make sure there is something going on there. We also need to consider the structure of the story and to make sure we are using the tools we've collected in earlier chapters and all the other elements you will come across as you continue writing.

Consider the following points and check that you can address them, whether to add to your story or realize that they don't fit with what you are writing:

- Make sure to use all the senses when appropriate.

- Understand what the character's motive is, that there is a reason for how they act.

- Know what the driver of the story is: opposition or conflict.

- Decide where to start your story, as this will impact the structure.

- Sometimes we tell something: for example, he sat down. Other times we use the senses to show the action if we want to draw the reader in.

- Think about why you are telling this story. This will let you know what the point of it is.

- Our character must move on in the story, whether this is external or internal.

- Very important – do you want to read stories like the one you're writing?

Exercise

This short story outline, which is adapted from an exercise I was introduced to during my master's programme, is something I go to whenever I'm stuck. Even if I don't use the story it produces, it gets me writing and thinking about what I want to say. The first couple of times I would say follow the questions, then, when you've answered them, move things around for the edit so that it feels more natural.

Note that the final question opens the story up and should be the base from which you jump into the plot and the story and explore who the character is in the world you've invented. Answer the first eleven questions in two or three sentences but write whole pages for question 12!

I find it's useful if I write this story in the first person and the present tense, but I'm also aware that it is difficult to maintain the present tense when we're writing. Write in the point of view you are comfortable in and enjoy the process.

For example:

When I walk through the door my eyes are immediately pulled towards the large clock on the wall. I'm not sure if my eyes are playing games with me, so I close them, just for a second, but it feels wrong, so I open them again. The clock is still large and so loud. (First person, present tense)

She walked through the door, dragging her feet. Her eyes were immediately pulled towards the large clock on the wall. She gasped. She couldn't understand what she was seeing and briefly closed her eyes. Her skin prickled so she opened them again quickly. The clock was still large and the noise it was making was deafening. (Third-person limited)

I want you to imagine that your character is going somewhere they've been before, but this time they are alone and not quite comfortable with what they are about to do.

1   When they step in what do they see first? How do they feel about it?

2   Choose a time of day. What does it mean to the character and why?

3   There's a noise in the distance. What is it? Does it bother your character? Is it a familiar sound?

4   There's a very distinctive smell. What does it remind them of? Does it evoke a memory?

5   Pick something out of the setting that stands out to your character. Does it remind them of something? Is it something they want or something they hate?

6   There's something about their clothes that either feels right or wrong. What is it?

7   What have they got on their feet? Why would that matter?

8   They're carrying something. What is it?

9   Something feels out of place. How does your character know? What is it?

10   They see someone coming towards them. Who is it?

11   Show how it makes your character feel physically. What's their reaction?

12   What happens next?

Round up

Plot and story are important in our writing.

Creating tension keeps the interest in the story and hooks the reader. It doesn't have to be all action that creates the tension; it can be quietly internal. Our characters move from point A to B in some way.

We don't have to always start our stories at the beginning and follow it through directly. We can start after the climax and then unravel; we can start at the resolution and take the reader back.

Read

The following story, 'Mr Koala' by Malcolm Cocks, is quiet and is driven more by the emotion of the protagonist. You may need to read it a couple of times to see the plot and the story. Think about the who and the why, consider the emotional journey our protagonist is going on. Draw on the senses, character, voice and language. Notice how the story is revealed through reminiscence and mirrored in what is happening. Identify the story and the plot and think about how you would write a similar story.

'Mr Koala'

Malcolm Cocks

She had her work cut out that morning. The postman had left a little red card to say he would be attempting redelivery. Already there were several packages stacked against the walls. They had built up in the hallway, making it difficult for Millie to get in and out of the flap. There were also six smaller packages for pick up, labelled with black felt-tip in his neat unjoined writing. And she had her appointment that afternoon.

'It's like a flipping sorting office in here' she said to herself, pushing one of the larger packages with her foot until it sat flush against the wall. It worried her that one day one of the twins would call round and find her knee-high in mysterious packages. And who would receive the parcels when she went into the hospital for her surgery? We shall cross that bridge when the time comes Miss Rozie, he had said. But he had not been for days and yesterday she had to sign for two parcels with no name, just her address. If another one arrived like that, she would have to complain. He shouldn't take liberties. It took her for granted and placed her in a dubious light in front of the postman.

Upstairs she found herself staring into the mirror again. It still shocked her to see the slack-jawed woman with thinning hair and skin that had begun to pucker round the mouth. But today she thought she looked less frayed. She cupped her hands under her breasts and pushed out with her chest to maximize the impression. She noticed them now like they were new. Then she sat on the bed and turned so that she saw herself in profile. She tried to squash the right one down to see how it would look. This did not make sense because she was getting a prosthetic. A friend from her Merton Mayhem Theatre Group had drawn her aside and confided to her in tragic whispers that nothing, nothing, could be worse for a woman. She had nodded and returned the pressure of the woman's squeeze, but secretly she thought, silly old goose, how does she know? It was the thought of what would happen when the cancer was gone that kept her awake at night and brought her to the mirror like this.

Perhaps she would feel differently after the surgery. But what she could not tell her friends from Merton Mayhem was that the cancer had been a lifeline. It had come like a call to arms and she had rallied. She had rallied and her determination had surprised her.

Asked how she would have responded to such news one year ago, she would have predicted exhaustion and defeat. In the aftermath of her diagnosis and in the build-up to surgery, the telephone had rung constantly. She had received cards and flowers and e-mails from people who had stepped out of her life decades ago. There was something to talk about again. She felt emboldened to call old friends and relatives and she was encouraged by their genuine interest in what she had to say.

She was also afraid. But even this was a new sensation. And so far, she had hardly suffered. There was little pain and she was sure in fact that her energy levels were up since the diagnosis. She had a new diet with new foods to prepare. She felt different, and it showed. In any case, the cancer had thrown her and Mr Koala together and she would be grateful for that always. Mr Koala and the cancer came into her life at the same time and a new rhythm was created for her. She was used to arranging her life now around these morning deliveries and the afternoon appointments. She looked forward to the evenings when he would stop by and was surprised to find how bitter the disappointment if he did not. She also looked forward to the appointments with her oncologist who always remembered her name and asked after Millie and the twins. She was secretly flattered that her doctor insisted she opt for prosthesis immediately following the surgery. He had even suggested that she consider having a nipple tattooed on to the reconstructed breast. They had tattoos for dark skin, too, he had reassured her.

She was proud of how she handled that discussion. The oncologist was a handsome man. That first time when he had walked into the waiting room to collect them, she had nudged her daughter in the ribs, partly out of genuine excitement but also because she knew it would make her indignant. She was still allowed to have urges. She had not escaped the parish busybodies in Grenada to be policed by her own pickney. When had Linda become so uptight? Linda and Andrew could never know about Mr Koala until things became official. She could not deal with a lecture and she did not want her son to make jokes at her expense.

She smiled at herself in the mirror now as she thought about her secret. She had always had a streak. It was the same streak that brought her to London from Grenada, knocked up with twins and no husband, all those years ago.

The breast had to go. She accepted this like she accepted most abstract facts. Her main regrets were for Mr Koala. This was jumping the gun. Things had not got that far yet. But it made her happy to think of it. She put on her best pout and hugged her arms around her chest. But without make up, the image depressed her. She should get dressed. Her tea had gone cold and the postman could ring at any minute.

When the doorbell did ring, it was not the postman. Two police officers, a young woman and a mild-eyed man greeted her in unison.

'Mrs Neckles is it, mam? Officers Sharpe and Motte, mam. We wonder if we could have word, please?'

'Ms. I never married.'

She took in the handcuffs that gleamed at their sides and the car that was parked across the road. She wasn't properly ready and felt exposed. They must have seen this because the woman police officer explained that she was not in any trouble, but they did have some questions for her about her neighbour at Number 80.

'Mr Koala? He's not been hurt, I hope?' She addressed herself to Motte but it was Sharpe who replied.

'Nothing like that, mam. Perhaps if we could come in for a minute, we'll explain.'

The voice was crystalline, but she could not be sure where it was from. She hesitated a moment, wondering what it could all be about and whether she should ask for some ID. But this seemed churlish, so she swung open the front door, grateful that she had been up early enough to give the sitting room a tidy, and hoping that no one from the neighbouring houses had seen two police officers come in. Rosemary decided that the man was definitely Motte. He moved slowly and had one of those mousy little moustaches which wiggled now and then, testing the air. Sharpe was brisker. Bright eyes sparkled beneath dark hair. A young chit. But everything about her said that she did not suffer fools lightly.

'I see you've got a lot of post there, Mrs Neckles?'

Motte plopped into the sofa so that Sharpe was obliged to sit down beside him. This was a relief. She would take the armchair in the corner so she didn't have to face them head-on. But first she needed to calm herself. She needed tea. Motte brightened at the mention of tea and his partner shot him a glance before saying a glass of water would be fine, thank you, mam. When Rosemary returned with the drinks, it was Sharpe who launched in.

'Right, Mrs Neckles. Earlier you referred to your neighbour as Mr Koala. Is that a different name he's been using?'

She had never learned his name. She thought that it had begun with a K and ended in L and A. And she knew there was a string of syllables in between.

'I'm really bad with foreign names, so I just called him Mr Koala,' she tried to explain. The moustache twitched. So she attempted to explain herself further.

'He's a short fellow, and slightly bow-legged. And he looks quite cuddly, with his beard and all. If you know what I mean?' There was no indication that they did, so she made a final feeble attempt.

'I mean he didn't mind me calling him that. The name suited his temperament. He said so.'

'I see, mam. Did he ever mention any other names? We think he might have used . . .'At this point she paused to refer to a small note pad. 'De Saram, Pala, De Silva, and possibly also Didiwallagi in the past. Any of those ring a bell?'

'Look, can I ask what this is about? I mean is Mr Koala . . . is my neighbor under arrest?'

'Unfortunately, mam, we are not at liberty to discuss the case with you. Let's just say that Mr Gokawallah is a person of interest at this time.' Motte sat nervously with that rabbity look. Sharpe took control.

The voice was relentless. She did not find its lilt at all comforting. It wanted to know whether she had not noticed anything strange about the comings and goings at Number 80? Had Mr Gokowallah ever borrowed money from her, or used her credit cards to make purchases online? How many people had she seen come and go next door? Any unusual smells? An increase perhaps in humidity?

The conversation passed in a blur. Rosemary had been taken off guard. What stuck in her mind as the voice went up and down in her front room was that she did not even know his name. She wished she had learned it.

She didn't know what it all meant, but somehow she knew not to say about the parcels. Or the damp that had taken hold in her loft since Mr Koala moved in.

A button had come loose on the armchair and twiddling it helped block out Sharpe's tinny voice. The twins were right: button-tufted sofas are asking for trouble. But it was nothing she couldn't take a needle to. Rosemary tried to focus on the button and the beige square of material around it. But she couldn't block out the scrape of the pencil and the voice like a bell.

'I am impressed you can talk and scribble in your ledger at the same time, officer Sharpe,' she heard herself say.

After every question Sharpe's head bobbed up to look her in the face and she knew she was being watched closely, in case she gave something away. She did not say much. She only shook her head, wanting them to be gone.

At last, the policewoman snapped the book shut and stood up. She handed Rosemary a card with a number and said to call in case Mr Gokowallah got in touch. She wanted to say, that's not his name. She wanted to tell them that he is a sensitive man. She wanted to show them the beautiful orchid he had grown for her. Motte was fumbling with something which he wanted her to take. In the end, he slid it across the table – it was a pamphlet that says 'Victim Support'. She wanted to scream. But there was no point making a fuss and it might be something to do later.

After they left, there was a tiredness like she had been throwing her body against the door to keep wild animals out. Her nerves were shattered. But her skin thrummed and her cheeks felt hot. She decided to spike her tea with a little rum to calm her down before the hospital.

She drank the tea leaning against the counter in the kitchen where she could see the orchid on the windowsill. The yellow flowers spotted with red, like the handkerchief of a consumptive. They are the size and shape of cats' ears and feel silky and cool between her finger and thumb.

'For you, Miz Rozie, with love from Sri Lanka.' It had come in one of those little brown pots. And he had showed her how to pot it and how much water to give. It was a special hybrid that his father had created, he told her. The orchid always made her think of her cancer, she told him once. This upset him. 'If my orchid reminds you of your bloody cancer, you must give it back or throw it out.' If it was not a cancer gift, then what was it? An initiation. Or a bribe? For weeks, nothing had happened in the little brown pot. She was ready to toss it out. But now here it was, bright and strong and unexpected.

Motte's pamphlet was waiting for her when she got back from the oncologist. There were little thumbnails of people having earnest conversations on the phone. In one, a young black woman, presumably one of the charity's typists or receptionists, smiled broadly at someone to her left. Everyone looks young and happy, apart from an elderly man on the back fold who looks embarrassed. His flabby cheeks droop like the wattles of a forlorn rooster and he looks as though someone tricked him into the photo. She folded the pamphlet into a book of Creole recipes she had brought from home.

She does not want a stranger's professional concern. She wants to hear his voice, the way he rolls the R in Rosie and says Z for S. The grunting that said he was listening. She wants to tell him that she does not care that there are no orchid bulbs in the little brown parcels, or that his import export business has nothing to do with tropical plants. She fingers the little bit of paper crumpled carefully in her purse. 'For emergency only please, Miz Rozie' he had said. The neat line of digits had begun to smudge.

She curled and uncurled the paper round her finger and, biting down on her lip, thought of the silly things women have done for love. She thought of the aunts in her parish in Grand Anse who sucked their teeth and wiggled their fingers in admonishment of her skirts, her first boyfriend, the pleasure she took in rum.

Then she imagined Linda's outrage and slapped her leg with glee. Being crab-walked in handcuffs to a waiting car, perhaps stopping only to touch Andrew on the cheek. *Rosie, girl, keep your head high and march out there like you done nothing to shame yourself*, she told herself. The *Wimbledon Guardian* would do a big spread. Merton Mayhem would make a play about it, she was sure. It might even make the *Gazette* back home. But none of this could compensate her for the life she'd planned with Mr Koala. Only this morning it had seemed as sure and solid as the bold cursive on the paper she kept folded in her purse for 'emergencies'. Well, this was an emergency of the heart. Whatever the trouble was, they could face it together, she would tell him.

When she finally dials the number, the other person hangs up with a soft click.

9

Writing self, writing other, writing Black

- Who is other?
- Why does it matter how we portray self and other on the page?
- How do we approach the page authentically?

It's now time to discuss how 'other' is written on the page. We will take into consideration who 'other' is in terms of the story we want to tell. We will explore the power balances between characters and where that power comes from. Without judgement we will explore where the information we have on the 'other' in our story comes from. Whether this is for a person of a different ethnicity, socioeconomic background, sexual orientation, or status within the world created. We will look at where stereotypes come from and how to avoid them and ask the Black writer if we are writing ourselves as 'other' and whether we need to decolonize how we think of our characters.

This chapter is the crux of why I am writing this book. It has come out of my years working in tertiary education and in the community. It is a result of how many publishing houses ask us to present ourselves on the page or in film so that we become 'authentic' for the reader/watcher. It is about challenging how we see ourselves and others and our representation as individual human beings rather than as a homogenous group of people who can only have one dimension.

It has been interesting to work in the Caribbean where an island can be made up of an incredible mix of different ethnicities and yet all can freely claim their identity as one people under the flag. In Western countries, no matter how many generations have been in a place, there often is a distinction between being of that country and being 'other'. We still sometimes come across that wonderful question, 'but where are you from?' Even if our accent is pure bred Northern England (just saying). Having said that, teaching creative writing in spaces with Black writers always has the same impact when we come to thinking about how we write ourselves and how we write other.

This is a crucial tool to pick up whether you are a Black writer or are writing Black characters. English literature has often taught us that anything outside of white English is very much other and does not have the same attention to detail that white characters will receive. And I know we can say this about any writer who writes stories, but this is for Black writers and characters and for us to take time to assess how we see ourselves and our characters. Whether we dance across the pages unbridled or sit quietly in the margins occasionally popping our head up, but quickly retreating.

Why are there differences with the way in which characters are portrayed? We are bombarded daily through the various media with how certain groups of people are. I distinctly remember in 2010 when students were rioting in nationwide protests against proposed cuts in education funding. There was a news report on TV and the reporter was in Moss Side, Manchester. Now this is one of the predominantly Black areas of Manchester and it has had its issues and problems in the past and we lived through that. However, the news reporter stood in Moss Side in 2010 to tell people that the riots were happening nationwide and throughout Manchester, but they were not coming from Moss Side this time. There was no reason whatsoever to include a mention of Moss Side in the report, but because the rioters were predominantly white, the network decided that the focus needed to be shifted. When we are bombarded with this type of representation in the mainstream, we ourselves can also buy into it. Even if we don't think it's us that are stereotypes, those others over there could be and if we're not careful we fall into the trap of othering ourselves.

There are preferences and prejudices between the groups no matter how many generations have lived in a place. An example of this is uncomfortable but worth considering as a Black writer. When we feel something deeply negative about white people, it is based on a history of the general. That is, a history that was politically, racially and brutally undertaken by the *majority* of white people in the West against pretty much everyone else in the world. Only it wasn't the *majority* of white people.

The majority were scraping a living doing menial jobs, had no schooling, were not involved in any decisions taken by the higher powers, whether that was Parliament or the monarchy. Should all white people be taken as the same in that case? Absolutely not. It is an uncomfortable discussion to be had, but it is important as writers that we get it right, that we understand where our opinions, prejudices, biases and all else comes from, whether negative or positive.

Often we can and do write our white characters, or our characters from the dominant group where we live, in full technicolour. There are many reasons for this. We are used to reading white characters, watching white characters in movies and on television. For many years, in the West, that has been the norm and unquestionable. There is also the fact that when we are in a minority, we have learned to observe the dominant other. We know how to behave, how to speak, how to accept our roles. This places us in a position that gives us an insight into our 'other' that is necessary for survival. Think back to period dramas, whether written or screened. The servants know every little thing about the people they serve whereas the aristocrats are constantly surprised by anything their servants can do. They don't need to understand or know about their servants whereas the servant has to know their employer through and through.

I was running a workshop many years ago and a participant was writing a story that was solid. The language and creole on the page worked excellently, the main protagonist was centralized and not given hero status, but was a three-dimensional Black character telling her own story. Then another character entered. This character was from another country, English was not her mother tongue, but she knew enough to get by. However, the participant had written this character in caricature. The voice was childish, using toddler-speak broken English and the character herself was a stereotype of a working woman from a particular socio-economic background. There was no substance to her. That's not to say that all characters are as important as the main protagonist and should have equal share in a story – our stories would become very long in that case. But the character should have been fully developed before she strolled onto the page, and she should not have been a stereotype. I gently pointed out that this character had moved countries, she was an economic migrant, she was working, looking after her family and was bilingual. This character deserved respect on the page and not to be exploited as childish and uneducated.

We often come across explanations such as 'but that's how "they" speak'. That's what 'they' do. As writers, that is not good enough as an explanation. If we do not want to be othered on the page, why would we do this to our characters who are different to us. There are always ways to present our characters on the page (look back at the language chapter) and we should take care to do this.

Discussion point

- Why do we have to think about how we portray ourselves and others on the page?

- How do we write about ourselves and others?

- Where do stereotypes come from?

- Challenge yourself about things you know about groups of people and then work out where those stereotypes come from.

Example 1

Blind people hear and taste and smell what other people cannot, and what Ma Taffy smells on this early afternoon makes her sit up straight. She smells it high and ripe and stink on the air, like a bright green Jackfruit in season being pulled to the rocky ground below. The smell is coming down John Golding Road right alongside the boy-child, something attached to him, like a spirit but not quite.

KEI MILLER, *Augustown*, 1

This example shows how the author has written a character who is more than the fact that she cannot see. He has employed the senses and has written 'other' in a believable and acceptable way.

Example 2

Rusi's laugh was special, a spectacular performance. First a grunt, deep in her chest, *ggrumph*, as if she was mad about something, then a louder guffaw, once, paced out. More silence as she gathered her breath and energy, grimacing as though she had a bellyache, as if the joke was killing her, and then, just when you thought it wasn't going to happen this time, she really was mad, the volcano erupted, the tornado, the hurricane! There was nothing else to do but giggle as I watched her with awe and some apprehension.

DOREEN BAINGANA, Tropical Fish (2005), 3

I chose this example to show how fully formed the author has made Rusi, who is a house girl with no status. It would be easy to dismiss her and to simply have things happen to her in passing. Instead, Rusi has been brought alive on the page by the narrator who sees her.

Example 3

After a while, Larissa got up and washed her face, straightened her clothes, and walked with me back to the house to resume her duties. My parents must have spoken to her, but she took no time off. I didn't see her cry that day or any other. She never mentioned her sons.

And something comes to me now that would never have occurred to me then: how when the son of one of my parents' friends had died, his mother had been treated so tenderly by everyone, the drama of his illness and death freely shared, the funeral a community event.

OLIVE SENIOR, The Pain Tree (2017), 10–11

This example stands out and is important. Olive Senior is a Black Jamaican writer, her protagonist in this story is white. The example refers to a time when the maid's son is killed during the war and the narrator reads the telegram to her. Senior has captured beautifully the different characters and their positioning. She shows how the maid,

Larissa, is a non-person, not worthy of being shown in 3D. Not because Senior thinks so, but because that was how Larissa was perceived by the family she worked for.

There are many examples in literature of where Black characters are not afforded the space and the respect to be fully functional on the page. Mainly written by white writers who cannot see a Black character as anything but a stereotype. We as Black writers can and must do better, by questioning ourselves and understanding the complexities of othering, whether that is our Black characters or any character we have in our stories.

Exercise 1

For this exercise you are going to take a long hard look at yourself.

You will define yourself as a fully three-dimensional character. Don't skip the rough bits, we are all shadow and light. What is the balance of power you hold? This can be in your home, at work, any place you frequent and mix with other people. This is not an easy question to answer, but it is important for us, as writers, to understand what makes a fully formed character.

- Write a character profile for yourself (look back at chapter 4).

- Really enjoy producing yourself on the page.

- Write everything you know about yourself. Childhood friends, firsts, the things you've done and why, the things you wished you'd done and why you didn't. Spend time excavating what makes you who you are.

- Once you're happy with your character (you), place your character in a situation with a group of other people who are not the same – this can be due to race, sexual orientation, age, disability, economics. For example, an office where your character is the manager (or the cleaner), a classroom, a cruise ship. Use your imagination. Create a scenario where your character has to interact with others.

- Let your character react and be aware of how you write the 'other'.

Exercise 2

Write a character who isn't you. This character could be male/female, Black/non-Black, differently abled/able bodied, gay/not gay, old/young, rich/poor. Note that these are binaries, and our characters, just like us, are rarely one thing or another.

Think about people you know, do some basic research about the character you choose to write.

Choose a short scenario and put your character in it.

How comfortable does it feel?

Have you made the character believable?

Have you allowed the character to simply be on the page?

Round up

We must take care how we present ourselves and others on the page.

We must avoid stereotypes and understand who our character is and make them three-dimensional. Challenge ourselves constantly about how we portray our characters and why, consider who holds the balance of power.

And finally, forget all about this worrying matter when you are writing your first drafts because editing will take care of any glaring issues.

Read

The following story, 'Strike', follows Selena, a recent immigrant to the UK, and some of the struggles she goes through. Notice how she navigates her way around the other characters in the story. Ask whether she is othered in the story or if she takes up space. Look at how Iliana is represented. Notice how Mary, as a Black character, is portrayed as being flawed. Think about your own writing and how your characters interact with others.

'Strike'

Muli Amaye

Sitting in the dark café bar looking around, her heart was still beating a little fast but that was good. It meant that she would stay alert. In the back of her mind the words 'not long, not long' that had been shouting were still playing to the rhythm that had been her footsteps, softer now, blending with the saxophone that was lisping from the speakers.

The table in front of her was sticky, with rings of sugary coffee where mugs had been carelessly placed. Selena held onto her red, leather bag as though it was keeping her afloat. Pressed against her thighs she could detect the lumps and bumps of her life that were packed away inside it. Her panties rolled small in one corner, her toothbrush and Vaseline body cream in the plastic wash bag, next to the green Palmolive soap wrapped in her face cloth. Two T-shirts that she'd picked up on Camden market and her old jeans completed the list of her life.

It was not the bag she had arrived with. That had been a cloth one that Nuna had made for her. She'd grabbed what she could before being driven away from the village in the back of the lorry. That bag had not survived The Centre, the pulling and dragging of belongings that was a constant. When she got out, she felt as though she'd left a little piece of Nuna behind. Nuna who had insisted she go, who forced her almost because she was terrified of what would happen to Selena if something happened to her. Of course, Selena hadn't known that then. She hadn't believed it could be so serious.

A tired looking waitress worked her way through the near empty café, wiping tables, picking up rubbish, slamming chairs. When she reached Selena she smiled, coolly.

'Coffee, love?'

She spoke loudly, as though not expecting Selena to understand. Her accent was thick and guttural, and Selena briefly wondered which East European country she came from. Her badge said 'Iliana'.

'Cappuccino. Please. Small.'

Iliana's smile dropped and Selena detected distaste in the slight elongation of the space between her nose and lip. Nuna would have said 'you smell shit, eh?' But Nuna wasn't here, and Selena simply lowered her eyes to the table and looked at the smears the dirty rag had left behind.

While she waited for her coffee, she looked at the clock on the wall opposite. It was old fashioned, like the clock her father had sent to Nuna years ago. Brown, plastic wood housing Black plates with white numbers that moved like flicking dominos. Selena had spent hours lying on her mat watching time drop down, the teasing of the numbers as they waited to fall and the click each tile made fascinated her. When they took the electricity, it didn't work anymore. 'Ahh, so time has stopped?' Nuna asked.

Selena wanted time to stop or to go backwards. She wasn't sure which. If it stopped, she'd be stuck here, now, forever. If it went backwards, she'd be safe, with Nuna. She played with the idea that it could both go backwards to where she wanted to be and then stop, so she would never arrive at where she was.

The coffee cup being noisily tipped onto the table in front of her brought Selena back. It worried her sometimes how her mind could wander along paths that didn't make sense. Nuna had called it waking-dreams and when Selena tried to correct her, to tell her the word was daydreams Nuna insisted that wasn't what she meant. Daydreaming, she said, can only be as good as what you know. Waking-dreams, though, were so big and wide you couldn't control them. Waking-dreams could go anywhere and do anything and be anything.

'I said, that will be £2.40. Please.'

'Oh, sorry, sorry.'

Selena opened the clasp on the front of her bag. Seeing the interest of Iliana she turned the bag around, with difficulty, bumping it against the table and spilling her coffee into the saucer. They both watched the brown liquid seep into the packet that held the sugar cubes. Iliana sighed, a sound that held a full conversation and none of it nice. She unceremoniously lifted the cup and placed the serviette on the saucer. The single caramel biscuit crumbled in its cellophane packet. This was how Selena had served coffee in the office. Before. When she was somebody. When she'd lived in town and worked for the Minister. They had the same biscuits. Imported from Italy.

Drawing out her purse Selena pretended not to have noticed the drama playing out on the table in front of her. She just wanted this Iliana person to go away and leave her alone. Pulling a five-pound note from the side of her purse, without opening it she smiled with her mouth as she handed it over. The waitress cocked her head to one side, looking like an enquiring cow in the village square. Selena pretended not to notice. She wouldn't tip somebody so rude, even if she could afford it.

There were two ways she could go now, and they had to be considered carefully. Selena needed some help. When she was a small girl whenever she had to choose, she would ask Nuna to help her.

'Nuna, please, I beg-o. Help me to choose.'

'*Hei*, this child' she would say, 'what if I was not here, *eh*? What if you were all alone and you had to decide quick-quick? Would you sit down and cry tears of beg-o?'

It was the strike that had brought her here, now. She hadn't thought it through. It hadn't registered that she might not be able to get down there. Since the first time she had been on the underground, Selena had been drawn to it. She had imagined sliding from the platform and delving into the darkness of the tunnel, being sucked into the dense emptiness, invisible, blind. When she had heard about the strike it was a sign, she had to be there. She had to swim into that absolute silence, out of sight, undetectable. She hadn't realised it would be so difficult to get there.

It seemed the right thing to do at the time. Going down, down, down into the Underground and the rush of warm air that tugged at her extensions as she rounded the corner for the platform. Sometimes she stopped just there and let her hair whip into a frenzy, lashing at her face. Jostling bodies would move her along and then there it would be. The tunnel. Calling to her. Promising peace.

The pain that had been her constant companion for weeks now tightened and winced inside of her. Selena pulled her bag closer, wrapping her arms around it, holding her life together. Nuna was gone. Selena didn't know if she could survive any longer. She was tired. The past year had been so hard and so different. From the language that she thought she was so good at to the way people walked in the street or lived in one room. That had been the most difficult. Living in one room with that woman. She had been wicked, and Selena was glad that she would never have to see her again.

When she had first contacted Mary, Selena was so happy that she had found somebody she knew. Back home, when Mary's sister was finishing school, it had been Selena who helped to place her in the Minister's office. Mary rang her and begged that she give her small sister a chance. Because Selena did not have her own brothers and sisters to look out for it had been easy. She had groomed the girl well into how she should attend the interview. Had chosen the dark suit from her own wardrobe and dressed the girl. And this was how Mary repaid her.

At first it had been wonderful. They'd hugged and laughed. Mary took her to church and introduced her to all her friends. She even found Selena a job working in the hospital. Of course, Selena had no papers to work so Mary gave her own, just temporarily, just to get her on her feet. Selena went out every evening at 8 p.m. She took the Underground, Victoria Line, Northern Line, walked to the hospital and into the laundry. Loading the industrial machines Selena asked herself what she was doing. Why she was working in a job such as this when she had her HNC, she'd worked as a manager, wore smart suits, and had a good apartment.

Mary's room was small with one double bed pushed into the corner and no other furniture. They slept there together on the nights that they were both not working, and Mary did not allow Selena to move from the bed. Squashed up against the wall she often needed to place her hands between her legs to hold in the wee that threatened to squeeze out. Mary would punch her if she moved too much, and Selena found it hard to believe that she was reduced to living like that.

That was not the worst of it though. When she finished work at 6 a.m. there were some mornings that she wasn't allowed to return home. That girl-o! *Hei!* Mary had a boyfriend who occasionally, when she could force him to leave his wife, would come over and stay. On those mornings Selena would sit on train stations shivering. Her body would rattle like an old car suspension hitting potholes. *Hei*, she could die there-o! Not trusting that she wasn't being watched she would not stay in one place for too long or too often. Using her oyster card, she'd take the over ground and sit on different stations with the pigeons, waiting for cafés to open so that she could buy a hot coffee. It was there, on the station in Wandsworth that she found her next job. That saved her life. It meant that she could finish work at the hospital, take the train straight and be in a warm house.

The woman, Celia, said she didn't need to start until 8 a.m. but Selena arrived at 6.45 on a regular basis. Looking after the old lady, Grace, was a blessing. When she slept at 11.00 so did Selena. Just for an hour or two. But in comfort, stretched out on the sofa with a cushion under her head and a blanket covering. If she wanted to get up and go to the toilet she could. Just stand straight up and go there. Check on the old lady and then lie straight back down again.

Celia was upset when Selena said she had to leave. Tried different ways to make her stay, offering more money, saying how happy her mother had become, that it was all down to Selena and the way in which she treated her. Selena felt bad. She had entered into Grace's silent world. Often, they would sit and look at each other and Grace would tell Selena stories with her eyes and the movements of her lined face and drought-dry hands. Occasionally a tear would slip silently down her face and Selena would respond with floods of her own. Other times Grace would place her hand in Selena's and sit contented, applying rhythmic pressure with her middle finger to a tune that couldn't be heard.

Celia had also remained silent. Selena reasoned that she knew she didn't have papers, couldn't really work. And there was she, a solicitor. A good judge of character, she'd said. Selena provided what she needed and that was why she hadn't asked too many questions. There was no harm being done and she often told Selena that the alternative was to place her mother in a soulless place with strangers, to remove her from her own home. Even this could not change Selena's mind. She had to go.

Picking up the spoon she began to squash the parts of the sugar cubes that hadn't turned to liquid. She lifted the biscuit in its cellophane and crumbled it a bit more. Selena wasn't kept in The Centre for long. Her papers were good quality. And they were true. She was in danger. She had to run. England was the only place she could come to. This is where her father was. Or had been. She wasn't quite sure.

The others were being picked off one by one. The ones she'd met in The Centre. She couldn't recall the names they had used when they arrived, all the guys choosing different footballers' names, Ashley, Ryan, Paul. The girls choosing singers' names, Cheryl, Britney, Cher, as though somehow, they would matter if they had the right label. They'd all stayed in touch; met at the place where they had to sign in, fear holding them upright in the queues, chaining them together. Until one by one they stopped appearing and nobody spoke about them again. Instead, each signee carried the same thoughts, what if this was the day they discovered they had violated an unspoken piece of legislation? What if the people checking up on them had been in a fight with their wife or husband the night before? It was that easy to be detained. To be removed. To be given a life sentence. So, they changed their names, these fellow peace seekers. They changed their names and became somebody else.

Selena had not changed her name. Nuna had named her. This was who she was. It would be a betrayal to take away the one thing she had been left with when Nuna went. Is that what happened? Did Nuna simply go? Selena's heart increased its rhythm and she forced herself not to go there. She couldn't afford to lose it here on the station, to draw attention to herself, to have security looking at her, for her. No, no, no. She had to stay strong. She was Selena. She was the moon. That's what Nuna had told her. You are the moon. You control the seas. You hold the night together.

Selena became aware that she was being watched. It was almost as though an invisible hand was hovering over her hair from behind. She kept her body completely still, muscles tense. Waiting. Her eyes flicked to the clock; it had only been 15 minutes since she arrived. He couldn't have found her. The air behind her moved and she caught the smell of the waitress. Gripping her bag tightly she rose from her chair and made her way to the door, leaving the £2.60 change on the table. Keep your head down, Nuna always said. Don't draw attention to yourself. Straight back, eyes lowered, walk with grace. Selena reached the exit of the café bar before she dared to turn around. The waitress waved and offered a warm smile. Selena nodded once and walked on.

There were still decisions to be made. Selena had to concentrate. Her mind had been doing this a lot lately, wandering, back to Nuna. It was the silence that did it. There was nobody to talk to, nobody who she could trust. Mary had told her there was no choice. That the man she had brought back to the room was the only way she could continue to live there. That there were bills to pay, that she wasn't contributing enough. Selena could hardly believe what she was hearing. She could not imagine what had made her old school friend so evil. She was pleased that she hadn't mentioned her other job.

Every week Selena went shopping and brought home enough food for them both, she added money to the gas and electricity keys, even though Mary would not allow her to use the fire. Selena paid her way and had no intention of lying down with that old man. His slobbering thick lips were parted in anticipation, and he rubbed the side of his jaw with thick fingers. Without a word she had picked up her red, leather bag that through habit was always packed ready. Pushing past them both she ran. He was quick for an old man and grabbed her arm as she reached the door. Pushed onto her so she brought her knee up, sharp, just like Nuna taught her. He fell and she ran.

She hadn't intended to reach Euston station; Angel was her destination when she jumped on the bus. Angel, with the longest escalator in the Underground. Selena didn't know if this made it the deepest because sometimes, she had to go down once and then down again in other stations, but the thought of slipping vertically into the middle of the earth appealed to her.

She had soon realised that this wouldn't be possible. Each Underground station the bus passed was shuttered or gated. An occasional burst of workers with placards were evident, although they looked more like a group of friends chatting over a cigarette break than a serious picket line. Selena felt as though her own life had been on strike for the past year, her tongue was weighed down with placard slogans.

Hoisting her bag onto her right shoulder, she wandered over to the back of the station her slow steps and exaggerated looseness in her shoulders lying about the way she felt inside. The escalators were still, and the security guard raised one eyebrow at her as though inviting her to speak. Selena walked straight past and out the door. The smell of coffee and donuts from the temporary looking kiosks greeted her and she hesitated. It was early. People everywhere were walking with purpose, had somewhere to go. Selena had nowhere. She knew that. Turning quickly, she walked back into the station. Looking at the screen she saw that the next train was for Manchester Piccadilly. At the ticket machine she touched the screen, fed in the money. She was crossing the line.

10

Writing Black emotion

- Consider how we approach emotional writing.

- Ask the question of whether it's necessary and why.

- Work out how to do it in a safe way that works with our stories.

Emotion is essential for stories to be engaging and we need to understand how that emotion is reflected within the story. Black people, in the diaspora, grow up with microaggressions that affect how we view ourselves and our place in the world. This feeling is extended to countries with predominantly Black people, as globalism and the after-effects of colonialism impact lives daily. How we harness the emotions we encounter and allow them to flow through a story enables us to produce writing that impacts without overwhelming. We have to find ways to create the distance necessary whilst still retaining an emotionally charged story.

Black writers are often expected to produce stereotypical characters who will be moody, loud, aggressive, suggestive. The emotions attached to these types of stereotypes can be seen in movies and on television screens, can be read about in mainstream media to show 'how we are'. It is our job as Black writers to challenge this. To understand that we are fully functional human beings with the whole range of emotions available to us as everybody else on the planet. Therefore, our characters get to be fully functional on the page, too.

As writers we often avoid going too deep with the emotional aspect of stories, not knowing that we are avoiding it or why. When we're young, or beginning writing, we can go too deep into the emotional side of stories and lose the plot and story to the emotion. But because we're feeling it so deeply, and want the reader to experience the same, we feel the sacrifice is worth it. Honestly, it probably isn't worth it. We need to create balance and produce stories that explore the world we create and the world we live in and allow space for our characters and our readers to feel their way through it. As writers we use emotions that we are aware of, whether our own or those that have impacted us from reading or research. We take the emotion and shape it into something that readers can connect with.

There are ways we can create emotive stories without going into lurid details. Often the emotion of our characters is shown through actions. If our writing isn't emotional the reader will not connect. Our writing can only be as emotional as we are. Even if we hide our emotions, the fact that we write means we have them. We just have to tap in. A participant in a workshop many years ago, who was an excellent writer, decided that they would only write light-hearted romance. There was a reasoning in their mind for this. Their job demanded that they listened to people's pain daily and it took a toll on them. Therefore they decided that light-hearted romance was as far as they could go emotionally, in order to protect themselves. I understood this completely, and never pushed the writer. We had spent many weeks together by that point and there were many weeks to go. So we had built a rapport. By getting to know them and understanding their needs, we were able to negotiate a space where they felt safe to express their characters' emotions. This added a depth to the romance stories and gave the characters a solid three-dimensional way of being. The writer felt safe and the stories blossomed.

When our characters are emotionally invested in something, they can have tunnel vision. We as the author need to know that they are invested yet look at them as a specimen in a petri dish and observe what has made them as emotional as they are. Then make sure that the reader, while being involved with the character, can see around them too. This takes practice and experience, but it is definitely worth mastering to take our writing to another level.

Example 1

On top of the double-decker, Ornella shifts uneasily. The top should be reserved for the young and their secrets. At forty-seven she was too old for this.

She breathes in deeply, counts to ten, then lets out a long airstream through her nose. She looks around self-consciously. Two boys with big earphones lounge at the back. They nod rhythmically. For a moment her heart stumbles; a small current of panic spirals up her throat. Is it, is it? She squints at the familiar red cap. *No, it's not my son.* Sweat beads trickle down her nose.

AKILA RICHARDS, Secret Chamber, in
Glimpse (2022), 161

This opening to the story provides the reader with a strong emotion that we can feel for the character. Even though we don't know what exactly is happening the writer has captured the tension and panic that Ornella is feeling.

Example 2

My mother danced all night and Roberta's was sick. That's why we were taken to St. Bonny's. People want to put their arms around you when you tell them you were in a shelter, but it really wasn't bad. No big long room with one hundred beds like Bellevue. There were four to a room, and when Roberta and me came, there was a shortage of state kids, so we were the only ones assigned to 406 and could go from bed to bed if we wanted to. And we wanted to, too. We changed beds every night and for the whole four months we were there we never picked one out as our own permanent bed.

TONI MORRISON, *Recitatif* (2022), p xxxix

The emotion in this example is subtle. The emotion is in the things that are not being said. It is written in the past, so the narrator has the distance, but the suppressed emotion is evident in the scene. In the 'people want to put their arms around you' and the 'shortage of state kids' and the way that 'we never picked one out as our own permanent bed'.

With practice we will get ourselves to a point where we can take emotions that we have felt in certain circumstances and give them to our characters in ways that fit into the plot of the story. The emotion is real, but the circumstance is very different. In this way we are not inserting ourselves into the stories but are ensuring that our stories and characters have life and emotion that motivates and enhances the story. Writing in this way ensures that we are not exposing ourselves as the writer and yet we are still giving our character and story the full experience.

Discussion point

- How important is it to write emotion into our stories?
- If we write subtly and concentrate on the story, can we still show emotion?
- How do we place distance between ourselves and the writing?

Exercise 1

Often, we feel that big emotions are the only emotions worth writing about or including in our stories, but that isn't the case.

Think about a time when you were emotionally invested in something and could only see from your own perspective – possibly young childhood. It can be something as simple as wanting a toy so badly that it's all you could think about for months. It was something that young you really desired. If there is nothing that comes to mind, imagine it.

It's your birthday or Christmas and you're opening a wrapped gift and it is: a) the gift of your dreams, *or* b) a poor substitute

Write a paragraph about it. Remember or imagine that longing, the excitement building up inside, the hours spent dreaming about riding that blue bike or bouncing that special edition basketball. What about that doll, the one in the shiny packaging with all the accessories that you could get to go with it? Ruminate and write all of that emotion on the page. Build up to opening the gift and explore the feeling when you see it.

Exercise 2

Now you are going to write about the same incident from another person's perspective. This can be a parent or caregiver, teacher, aunt, sibling, and so on. This only works if it's someone who is invested in the giving of the gift. If it's a parent, did they save for months to purchase it, or did they not have the funds at all? Did the teacher know you wanted the purple pencil case but had forgotten and given you the green one instead? Had you gone into the shop every week and the shop owner knew how much you wanted the item but had sold the last one before it could be bought for you?

This paragraph is completely from the giver's perspective, so you must imagine how they feel about the gift. It is what they think and feel that is important in this scenario.

Exercise 3

The following exercise builds on the previous two exercises. Having explored your own emotions and imagined those of the gift giver, we can now practise placing emotions in a different scene.

Think about an emotional place you've been in. Often we will immediately think of something terrible that happened to us and as Black people I'm sure we can call on many incidents of racism, microaggressions or acts of violence. And often this is expected of us for our characters. This falls into stereotype and does not allow us or our characters to run the full gamut of being human. So for this exercise, feel free to tap into a happy emotion, one full of joy, but also feel free to tap into something dark. This is your exercise to do in your way. Our emotions are allowed a full range of being.

Tap into that feeling. Sit with it for a little while. You will then give the feeling, not the circumstance to a character. For example, if the emotion is intense pleasure for a meal you had, give that to your character for an exercise programme they have completed. If that emotion is from the break-up of a relationship, take that emotion and let your character feel the loss of a job they thought was going to see them through to retirement. You can use any deep emotion and replace the scene. Write a paragraph with your character feeling that emotion within a scenario that is relevant to them. Nobody needs to know where the emotion came from, but only how it is manifested in the writing and for the character.

Round up

Our writing needs emotion to make it live on the page and for our stories and characters to live and breathe. We must take care not to expose our own emotions on the page by taking a known emotion and giving it to a different circumstance that fits the character and the story.

Read

The following short story has emotion running through each paragraph. It is in the gaps in between the words, the way in which the narrator passes over information. For example, the mention of Mama is fleeting and it could easily be missed, but there is the feeling of loss each time she is mentioned. There are many more instances with subtle references to deep emotions. As you read through, try to identify the feelings behind the words.

'The First Shampoo
Hair Show'

Nii Ayikwe Parkes

Because the soles of our shoes cannot be allowed to wear unchallenged, we stand at the corner near Ma Lizzie's bakery, while Gyasi hammers curved metal heel protectors that look like horseshoes onto their clean elastomer surfaces. We know the shoes have elastomer soles because in school one of the rich boys bragged about his leather soles and another boy, a joker and genius footballer called Abebrese, took off his own battered shoes and countered, 'Well, mine are elastomer. When you have a longer word than that come back and brag.'

Our shoes are black, with rounded fronts like the nose of the plane they came from as a parcel from Mama, who works in a hospital in Eltham, London, while studying for an advanced midwifery certificate. Mine are two sizes smaller than my older brother's – except for that, they are identical, although his, like mine, are two sizes too big. This is why they need protection; they are forward-looking shoes, we are meant to grow into them, they speculate on our constant elongation into manhood.

'We have the new ones some,' Gyasi informs Da casually, as he hammers the final horseshoe onto Yaw's sole. 'The kind we put at the front of the sole.' He points to emphasize. 'They are good paa.'

From the corner of my eye, I see Yaw grimace, as though imagining the extra noise he will make when walking down the hallways in school.

Da's hands tighten on our shoulders, which means that he is thinking about it, weighing the shoe-lifespan benefits against the cost. He turns to me. 'Kojo, what do you think?'

I shrug. It doesn't really matter since almost everyone at school has heel protectors and the hallways are a constant percussion of chaos anyway.

'I think it's a great idea,' says Da, taking off his own shoes to hand to Gyasi to upgrade, his socked feet etching striated footprints in the red dust road.

Yaw doesn't say a word as we walk back home. We have all become quieter. We queue to buy bread on Tuesdays, we queue for cooking oil and maize once a month, we trek to Food Distribution Corporation in the industrial area with chits when we hear they have a new consignment of rice. These are all contemplative activities. People smile in the queues, but they don't laugh. When you only eat once a day, you save your energy for the very best laughs. That's what Yaw told me two days ago when we were in our bedroom reading. That made me laugh.

Da walks about three paces ahead of us, occasionally saying something over his shoulder to keep our spirits up. He has been doing this since he called us to an early morning meeting to explain to us that the only way he could promise to feed us every day was if we only had one meal a day. We were not surprised. All our friends at school were already eating one meal a day. Da had held out longer than most families and we were sure he'd done it by eating less himself.

We can't tell him that we supplement our evening meal by foraging for wild fruits in the vicinity of our school at break times. We are not even sure what we are eating. We trust the friends who tell us they are edible, but we still nibble at the edges of these bright sweet and sour mysteries, wait a few seconds for our bodies to accept them before we devour them. Our friends come from all over the country, some are from farming and hunting villages – this is how they know things that we don't. Once, after school, six of us – including Abebrese, the joker – went out with catapults and killed three pigeons. We wrapped them in akokobesa leaves, cooked them in the ground whole, their feathers giving off smoke that made us cough, until they came out smelling like heaven. Abebrese said we should have taken out the gallbladders before cooking them, but Yaw said pigeons don't have gallbladders. Still, the flesh was bitter around the stomachs of the birds, but we ate them anyway – even their heads.

We can't tell Da these things. He is a proud man.

His thin frame loses detail as the sun sets. He has a small, brown pouch under his left armpit that we call Ali Baba because he manages to extract unusual treasures from it. Like the chit from his boss that allowed him to collect two whole dressed chickens a couple weeks earlier. His lanky silhouette, left arm immobile, darkening before our eyes, is the shape we are meant to grow into. I hope my outline will not be as lonely. We don't know when Mama is coming back.

As we near the still-green hedge that surrounds our home, Yaw speaks. 'I can't even do Michael Jackson moves with my shoes. My feet slip all the time.'

I laugh. I have seen him trying. It's like watching a grasshopper dancing with horseshoes.

Da is silent. He pauses briefly before swinging open the wooden gate that marks the only break in the rectangle of our hedge. His head drops.

I stop laughing. I think I have laughed too much.

When we step off the sand of the path onto the linoleum tiles of the veranda, our shoes click in time and Da clicks his fingers. He transforms into a spinning, jumping machine. We have never seen him like this. He is making music with his feet, with a smile as wide as the one on the wedding picture that dominates our living room. He looks off-balance because he is still holding Ali Baba in place with his left arm while his right arm is all over the place. When he stops, he is out of breath.

'Yaw.' He puts his arm around my brother. 'You can still tap dance. I will teach you. Chale, these new protectors are great!'

He puts Ali Baba beside him on the low wall of the veranda and motions for us to sit with him. 'After the second world war, when I was a few years younger than you are now – I think, seven – an American soldier from New York came to live not far from us, by your grandma's house in Tudu. He saw me dancing in the street and called me. For one year, he taught me this kind of dance. He used to make me dance barefoot in front of his friends. Have I told you about the Nicholas brothers?' Da jumps off the wall. 'I have a tape.'

Da has a collection of Betamax video tapes with no labels. The Betamax player was a gift from his boss and we are not allowed to touch it. Da says if your boss is always giving you gifts, it is a sign that you are not being paid what you are worth. However, the Betamax player is rare. The tapes are from a childhood friend of Da's who is also an accountant but lives in Chattanooga in America.

So we sit and watch the Nicholas brothers for an hour or so and then Da teaches us the basic tap steps. I can tell even Yaw is happy. We forget we are hungry.

***

Some weeks later, Da returns from work and triumphantly produces from Ali Baba a white, green, and Black card that says 'The First Shampoo Hair Show '83'.

Yaw makes the kind of face that only an eleven-year-old can make. 'Don't you think it's odd that people should be thinking about shampoo in the middle of a drought?'

Da shakes his head. 'We are lucky to have these for free. Other people are paying 350 cedis per family for entry.' He opens the double-fold card to the page where, above a row of green stars, a swirl of blue ink, an ebullient scrawl, announces 'Free Refreshment'. Da has that big wedding smile again.

I feel my stomach move with the kind of anticipation I felt after the coup d'état, when we all cleaned the streets as though preparing to lay the foundations of a new country. Nobody expected the drought then.

'Fixed rules and dogma cannot apply successfully to all this diversity. Short hair, long hair, hard lines, soft lines – these are scarcely philosophies . . .' Yaw has taken the card from Da. He can't hold back his laughter as he reads the introduction text. 'They are no more than part of the artist's infinite variety of choice . . .'

Da smiles. 'You are laughing now, but that's the best meal you'll have until Christmas. We are not going for our hair.'

'But this sounds like an art show. Are you sure there will be real food there?'

'This ticket is from your auntie Sally. She knows the organizers.'

'Auntie Sally?' Yaw holds his head.

Auntie Sally is Mama's sister, but she is not known for her thoughtfulness. She only turns up on our doorstep when she needs something. Da says Mama's family has lived in Accra for three generations; none of them goes to the village anymore, so one of them was bound to become that way.

'What did she want?' Yaw and I ask at the same time.

Da laughs in spite of himself. 'Nothing.'

Yaw raises both eyebrows. 'Da?'

'OK. She wanted to know how I got the chicken. She couldn't take the invitation back when I told her it was a gift from my boss.'

We roll around laughing and I know this is one of the very best laughs, and that Yaw means it. Sometimes we don't mind it's just the three of us. Yaw and I have cooked yam with egg stew and Da is back from work to eat with us. We miss Mama, but we are fine. She would be proud of us.

When the morning of the hair show arrives, we rise early to do our chores. On Saturdays we scrub all the floors. I clean the toilet bowl by hand with a worn boot brush that has lost all the blue paint that gave it vibrancy before, and Yaw cleans the mildew growing on the grout between the bathroom tiles before coaxing the whole room into a shine. We keep the Vim cleaning powder in the corridor so we can both reach it. We do the louvre blades last, taking them out of their aluminium frames just as the sun is rising. We have hated Saturdays since the drought began – less food and more dust seems a cruel trick of fate – but today we are happy. We ferry the louvre blades outside and sit on the verandah steps, soapy water sloshing between us. When Yaw chuckles, I know he is thinking about Auntie Sally, and I chuckle too, leaning to bump his shoulder with mine.

Da wakes up humming the calypso song that Lord Kitchener wrote for our independence day, and we join him to drink last-day tea, which is reassuringly tasteless, meaning that Da will take out a new teabag tomorrow. He gives us dry biscuits, pale and perfect, with the last-day tea, leaving a teaspoon's worth of thick jaara at the bottom of our cups to finish breakfast with.

After all this, it is still only 9:00 a.m. and the First Shampoo Hair Show starts at 4:00 p.m. We have to curb our anticipation somehow. Da turns the radio on and, after some announcements informing us of gifts of yellow corn and sunflower oil from the West and Food Aid from the UN, we hear Flight Lieutenant Jerry Rawlings talking about perseverance and change and believing in better days coming. His voice fades into the background, but it is a comfort to us to know that someone cares enough about our hunger to ask us to persevere. And we see him on TV in the evenings; he is even thinner than Da. If better days don't come, the adults will disappear first, their shadows will swallow them, and then we will be sucked into the vacuum they leave behind.

Yaw grabs a book from the bookshelf and goes to read in bed. I stand outside and stare at lizards loping back and forth in the hazy boundary between the blinding sunlight and the shadows cast by our hedge. Da taught us how to start fires using sunrays and a magnifying glass, and I find myself wondering what lizards taste like, or chameleons. What color do chameleons turn when cooked? I head to the bedroom as well, take a cowboy comic from under my pillow, and get lost in the Midwest.

Da wakes us up at 2:30 p.m. to get ready. Normally, to get to the Accra Technical Training Centre, where the show is, we would drive through Industrial Area to Kwame Nkrumah Circle and up the Ring Road to Kokomlemle, but Da's car is low on petrol so we have to use a route with more downs than ups. That way, Da cuts the engine when the car is going downhill, puts the gear in neutral, and releases the handbrake. We glide.

Gliding actually feels better than driving because you feel you are winning something back from the world, but it is slow and you have to know the city well. Instead of going via Kwame Nkrumah Circle, we turn off between Tesano and Industrial Area, cross over the Nsawam Road into Alajo, via Kotobabi and New Town to glide downhill through Nima to Kokomlemle.

Da flashes his card at the gate and we are inside. There are hairdressers trimming and styling hair and a handful of pioneering customers are sporting Jheri curls, which is the new craze. All the stalls, banners, bunting, and posters are green and white, like the invitation card. It's like a paper, fabric, and plastic jungle. I remember that it is Christmas Day in eight days. That is why Da's chickens are still mocking us with their featherless wings from the depths of our freezer.

By 5:30 p.m., we have seen every hairstyle twice. We try to look interested, but Yaw and I have our noses tuned for food and even Da's eyes are keen as a leopard's as we lope back and forth between the school buildings and the show area, our heels and toes clicking each time we encounter concrete.

Da points at a poster. 'Look, they have entertainment later.'

'Is there a poster for the refreshments?' Yaw says.

Eventually, Da asks a green and white clad attendant where he can find Auntie Sally.

'I don't think she's here,' he says, 'but check that building.'

The nail on his index finger is too long, but we follow the path it suggests and come to a small, square building, painted white with black, wooden windows – and a door – in sharp contrast. Like our house, it is encircled by a hedge with a gap that serves as the entrance. As we walk through the gap, I hear a guitar and the gentle thump of a djembe drum. The guitar stops and starts one note, then a pause, then again.

Da knocks on the door with the flesh of his fingertips.

A woman with a severely coiffed perm opens it wide, with a smile. 'Can I help?'

Da pops his head round the door. 'Is Sally Amankwah here?'

'No, I think – '

Before she can finish, Da points at the buffet table in the middle of the room. I feel a rumble in my belly before the aromas register, as though my stomach has become more perceptive than the rest of me.

'Are those the refreshments?' Da asks, eyes fixed on the mounds of rice, gari fɔtɔ, roast chicken, fried fish, and salad distributed artfully on the sturdy wood table. We know this is what we have made our pilgrimage for.

'Are you performers?' asks the lady. 'This is for the performers.'

A moment passes, like the gap of silence after a baby falls before it starts bawling. The room darkens behind the woman, flushed by the phenomenon of sunset. I take one step back but Yaw steps forward – beyond Da – and nods. 'We are dancers.'

Yaw jumps with his percussive shoes and replicates Fayard Nicholas's smile perfectly. Da claps and leads with an opening sequence. Yaw copies him and I follow, past the bemused woman into the room. And we dance, turning to silhouettes. We dance to settle our stomachs.

Conclusion

As we write we learn more each time we put pen to paper or fingers to keyboard. We grow our craft and collect tools along the way that we can employ for our future projects.

This book is necessary. One of the main takeaways I intend is that we make our stories, our characters, our settings, our voices and every other aspect of our writing ordinary. We don't have to perform for the page, but rather write our authentic stories. We don't have to stress the Blackness of our characters and their emotions, but allow them to be on the page fully formed. I wish I had been privy to this information when I began writing. I wish I had understood that my characters have the right to exist on the page as fully-fledged as any story that I had read from mainstream literature.

I hope that writers will take away what has been written in the spirit it has been written. This book can be a starting point for Black writers and those who want to write Black characters in their work. It has been written with the hope that it will make us stop and think and question how we are presenting on the page.

I have used many 'how to' books over my writing and teaching career, but I have never read one that has consistently and purposefully addressed Black writing and how we can approach the page with examples by Black writers. This book looks at how we as Black writers write 'others' and this is something that we need to be aware of to ensure we don't fall into the stereotypes that so often are written for us.

This book fills a gap for Black writers of African descent and I am sure there will be more to come.

Bibliography

Adiche, Chimamanda N. *The Danger of a Single Story*. TEDGlobal, 2009.

Amaye, Muli. 'Streamlining', in *Closure*. Leeds: Peepal Tree Press Ltd, 2015.

Baingana, Doreen. *Tropical Fish*. Amherst: University of Massachusetts Press, 2005.

Bell, J. and Magrs, P., eds. *Creative Writing Coursebook*. London: Macmillan UK, 2021.

Carter, Angela. *Wise Children*. London: Random House, 2012.

Danticat, Edwidge. 'Dosas', in *Everything Inside*. London: Vintage, 2019.

Danticat, Edwidge. 'In the Old Days', in *Everything Inside*. London: Vintage, 2019.

Daré, Abi. *The Girl with the Louding Voice*. London: Sceptre, 2020.

Evaristo, Bernadine. *Girl, Woman, Other*. London: Penguin Books Limited, 2019.

Gegele, A-dZiko S. *All Over Again*. Kingston, Jamaica: Blouse & Skirt Books, 2022.

Gyasi, Yaa. *Homegoing*. London: Penguin Books Limited, 2016.

Gyasi, Yaa. *Transcendent Kingdom*. New York: Alfred A. Knopf, 2020.

Hirsch, E. D. *Cultural Literacy: What Every American Needs to Know*. London: Vintage, 1988.

Hopkinson, Nalo. *Midnight Robber*. New York: Grand Central Publishing, 2000.

James, Marlon. *The Book of Night Women*. London: Penguin Publishing Group, 2009.

Kalu, Peter. 'The Fall of the House of Penhryn', in *Glimpse*. Leeds: Peepal Tree Press Ltd, 2022.

Kincaid, Jamaica. 'Girl', *New Yorker*, 26 June 1978.

Lloyd Bawo, Ayanna. *When We Were Birds*. London: Penguin Random House, 2022.

Lodge, David. *The Art of Fiction*. London: Random House, 2012.

London, Norrel A. 'Socio-Politics in Effective Curriculum Change in a Less Developed Country: Trinidad and Tobago', *Curriculum Inquiry* 27, no. 1 (1997): 63–80, DOI: 10.1080/03626784.1997.11075481.

McGrath, Ronnie. 'Contraband', in *Glimpse*. Leeds: Peepal Tree Press Ltd, 2022.

Miller, Kei. *Augustown*. London: Orion, 2016.

Mohammed, Celeste. *Pleasantview*. New York: IG Publishing, 2021.

Morrison, Toni. 'Unspeakable Things Unspoken: The Afro-American Presence in American Literature', in *Within The Circle*. Durham, NC: Duke University Press, 1994, 368.

Morrison, Toni. 'Recitatif'. Rochester, UK: Vintage Digital, 2022.

Onojaife, Karen. 'Here Be Monsters', in *Closure*. Leeds: Peepal Tree Press Ltd, 2015.

Owuor, Yvonne A. *Dust*. London: Vintage, 2014.

Persaud, Ingrid. *Love After Love*. London: Random House Publishing Group, 2020.

Ross, Jacob. 'Raising Tyrone', in *Tell No-one About This*. Leeds: Peepal Tree Press Ltd, 2017.

Ross, Jacob. 'The Understanding', in *Tell No-one About This*. Leeds: Peepal Tree Press Ltd, 2017.

Roy, Jacqueline. *The Gosling Girl*. New York: Simon & Schuster Limited, 2022.

Saro-Wiwa, Ken. *Sozaboy: A Novel in Rotten English*. Vancouver Island, BC: Pearson College Div, 1994.

Senior, Olive. 'Window', in *Discerner of Hearts*. Toronto: McClelland & Stuart Ltd, 1995.

Senior, Olive. *Dancing Lessons*. Ann Arbor, MI: Dzanc Books, 2014.

Senior, Olive. *The Pain Tree*. Leeds: Peepal Tree Press Ltd, 2015.

Simmons, Georgina. 'My Brother's Keeper', in *Shots in the Dark*. Manchester: Crocus Books, 2018.

Tutuola, Amos. *The Palm-Wine Drunkard*. London: Faber & Faber, 1977.

Short story contributors

Muli Amaye – 'Strike' (*Moving Worlds, A Journal of Transcultural Writings: Asylum Accounts* 12, no. 2 (2012)); 'Waiting' (*Tout Moun, Caribbean Journal of Cultural Studies* 4, no. 2 (2018)).

June Aming – 'The Water Beneath My Feet'.

Malcolm Cocks – 'Mr Koala'.

Peter Kalu – 'Getting Home: A Black Urban Myth (A Proofreader's Sigh)' (*Closure*, Peepal Tree Press, 2015).

Celeste Mohammed – 'Terre Brulee' (first published in *Adda Magazine*, 26 July 2024, by The Commonwealth Foundation).

Nadja Nabbie – 'Boss Lady'.

Courttia Newland – 'Underground' (*a book of blues*, Flambard, 2011).

Nii Ayikwe Parkes – 'The First Shampoo Hair Show' (first published in *Carve Magazine*, Spring 2015).

Leone Ross – 'Velvet Man' (*Come Let Us Sing Anyway*, Peepal Tree Press, 2017).

Index